rethinking your
supply chain strategy

rethinking your supply chain strategy

A BRIEF GUIDE

roberto perez-franco

MIT Supply Chain Strategy Lab
Center for Transportation & Logistics
Massachusetts Institute of Technology

Copyright © 2016 by Roberto Perez-Franco

All rights reserved. No part of this publication may be reproduced, distributed or transmitted in any form or by any means, including photocopying, recording, or other electronic or mechanical methods, without the prior written permission of the publisher, except in the case of brief quotations embodied in critical reviews and certain other noncommercial uses permitted by copyright law. For permission requests, write to the publisher, at the address below.

MIT Supply Chain Strategy Lab
77 Massachusetts Avenue, E40-293
Cambridge, MA 02139, USA
http://strategy.mit.edu
strategy@mit.edu

Rethinking your supply chain strategy/ Roberto Perez-Franco —1st ed.
MIT Supply Chain Strategy Lab — ISBN 978-0692666531

contents

introduction 7

the nature of the beast 9

our approach to the problem 15

a framework for rethinking SCS 23

capturing your SCS 33

a protocol for capture 46

evaluation criteria 63

applying the criteria 70

reformulating your SCS 92

reformulation examples 107

connecting the dots 118

references 123

index 124

*To the next generation
of supply chain practitioners*

introduction

If you are a supply chain manager, you may already know from firsthand experience that a variety of events can make you wonder whether it is time to revise your supply chain strategy. Be it internal changes, such as a revision of the company's business strategy or the launch of new products; or external changes, such as tighter regulations, disruptive technologies, or changes in the marketplace that disrupt the environment of the organization; or even the simple progression of a product along its life cycle: all these are events that require you to stop and reevaluate your existing supply chain strategy, to ensure it remains sound.

However, rethinking a supply chain strategy is not a trivial problem. Supply chains tend to be rather complex entities, and the act of thinking strategically about them, what we call supply chain *strategizing*, reflects this complexity. The absence of an established answer in the supply chain management literature regarding how to rethink the supply chain strategy of an organization further compounds what is already a daunting problem.

Between 2006 and 2016, a team of researchers at MIT's Center for Transportation and Logistics (CTL) explored the problem of supply chain strategizing, as part the Supply Chain 2020 Project. After a decade of research in collaboration with world-class organizations, significant progress was made. Many questions remain open, and will continue to be explored by an offshoot of the SC2020 Project, called the MIT Supply Chain Strategy Lab. But we feel it is time to share with the community of supply chain managers the insights we have derived so far on how to rethink the supply chain strategy of an organization.

That is the purpose of this text. Although it is still admittedly a work in progress, it encompasses a great deal of our thought on the subject. It is our plan to continue updating this tome as new projects are conducted and new questions are addressed. But, as a first version, it should do!

Acknowledgements

I would like to acknowledge the leadership and efforts of the founder of the MIT Supply Chain 2020 Project, Prof Yossi Sheffi, and of its first two directors, Dr Larry Lapide (2004-2005) and Dr Mahender Singh (2006-2011). I acknowledge also the contributions of the students that participated in the project under their lead, especially my dear friend and colleague Dr Shardul Phadnis. I would like to thank my colleagues at the Center for Transportation and Logistics, in particular Prof Sheffi, Dr Chris Caplice, Jim Rice and Ken Cottrill, for their constant support.

I also thank all the partner companies and organizations that engaged us in projects on the subject of supply chain strategy over the past decade: I appreciate your vote of confidence. I would like to thank my students and friends, who gave invaluable feedback on the method and on earlier versions of the manuscripts describing it, including this book, in particular Dr Daniel Mota, Dr Manuel Rippel, Javier Martin, and Dallas Ferraz.

Finally, as progress is made on the subject of supply chain strategy, I acknowledge the contributions of those scholars that have helped advance the field before us. I dedicate this effort especially to the memory of Dr Matthias Schnetzler – a brilliant supply chain strategy scholar whose life ended way too early – and to his loving parents, Bruno and Maya.

CHAPTER 1

the nature of the beast

Before we introduce you to our way of thinking about supply chain strategy (what we call 'our *philosophy*'), and present to you our way of tackling the problem of supply chain strategizing (what we call 'our *framework*',) let's discuss the nature of the problem that supply chain strategizing presents to supply chain practitioners.

The basic challenges

The first thing we must recognize about the problem of rethinking the supply chain strategy of an organization is that it presents not one *single* challenge, but a set of interrelated challenges. After many years working on the subject, we are convinced that, regardless of what approach you follow to tackle the problem of rethinking your supply chain strategy, you will face at least three distinct basic challenges, outlined in Figure 1 and discussed below.

Challenge 1: The first challenge is to *assess your current supply chain strategy*. By this we mean *both* knowing what supply chain strategy you have in place *and* recognizing its strengths and weaknesses. Understanding and evaluating the current supply chain strategy of your organization is fundamental, because – unless you are planning to scrap your whole supply chain – whatever you have in place today will likely serve as the starting point for any subsequent supply chain improvement effort.

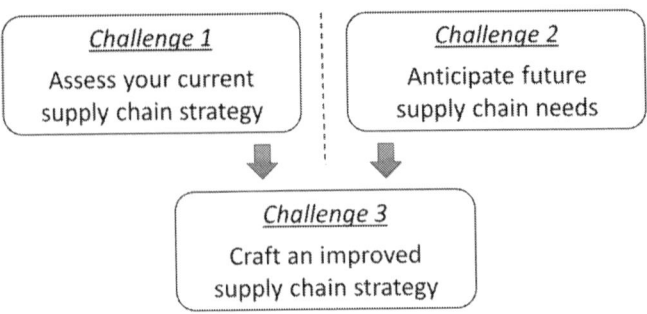

Figure 1: The basic challenges of rethinking a supply chain strategy

Assessing an existing supply chain strategy, however, is easier said than done, for two simple reasons. The first is that most supply chain strategies are not well defined: they are often left tacit or are poorly defined. The second reason is that often practitioners delude themselves into believing that their supply chains are doing today all sorts of nice things that – in reality – they are *not* doing, all while ignoring the very real detrimental things that are actually taking place.

Challenge 2: The second challenge is to *anticipate the future supply chain needs* that the organization may encounter. These needs will depend on factors under the control of the organization, such as the organization's competitive strategy and any corporate strategy guidelines that the supply chain will be expected to follow. But they also depend on factors beyond the organization's control, such as the market and the industry in which the company will compete, or – in the case of not-for-profit organizations – the environment in which they will operate.

Anticipating future needs is difficult because understanding the factors underlying them is not trivial: if it is difficult to understand an organization's supply chain needs in the present, trying to anticipate what needs the future may bring is even harder. Yet, since strategy is crafted for the future, we need a way to improve our understanding of what the organization's supply chain needs may be in the future.

Robust

Challenge 3: The third challenge is to <u>craft an improved supply chain strategy</u> for today and tomorrow. The new supply chain strategy must support the expected future strategy of the organization, and be able to function in the future environment of the organization as we have envisioned it. At the same time, this new supply chain strategy should retain or improve all the good features of the current supply chain strategy, while fixing as many of its weaknesses as possible. This three-fold goal, of fully supporting a new set of objectives while at the same time alleviating its current shortcomings *and* making as few changes as possible to the current supply chain strategy, is a tall order. Due to the complexity of the challenge, it is very easy to create new problems as we try to fix existing ones.

It's complicated!

Another thing we must recognize about rethinking a supply chain strategy is that it is complicated! To be more specific, it is what we would call a *complex problem*, as opposed to a *well-defined problem*.[1] Let's see what this actually means in practice. A **well-defined problem** is one where:

- we know exactly what our desired outcome looks like, and
- we have a set of well-defined criteria to evaluate the outcome;
- we know exactly all facts are relevant to the problem; and
- we know all the ways in which we can intervene, and can predict with precision all the consequences of each intervention.

Furthermore, a well-defined problem is usually limited to:

- problems that are static (e.g. that remain unchanged unless we intervene), and to
- problems that are relatively easy to comprehend.

On the other hand, a **complex problem** is one where:

- multiple goals – often at odds with each other – are pursued;
- the desired outcome is stated in a relatively vague manner;
- we do not have clear-cut criteria to evaluate the desired outcome;

---

[1] This section and the next two are informed by the influential ideas of Dörner (1983).

- we do not know all the facts that are relevant to the problem; and
- we cannot predict the outcome of every possible intervention.

Complex problems often include:
- problems that are dynamic (e.g. where things may change even if we do not intervene), and
- problems that are relatively hard to comprehend.

Like most problems that matter in management (and in life), rethinking a supply chain strategy is nothing like a well-defined problem; instead, it has all the features that make it a *complex problem*.

Rethinking a supply chain strategy requires us to pursue multiple goals, on areas that are often entangled by trade-offs; goals that can seldom be stated in precise terms. We often lack specific criteria to evaluate whether the goals pursued by our supply chain strategy have been achieved. We certainly do not know all the facts that are relevant to the future environment where the supply chain will operate, nor can we predict with certainty the outcome of every possible decision we make regarding it.

Due to the continuous changes that take place in the environment of the organization, the problem of rethinking the supply chain is dynamic, not static: things will change in time, even if you do nothing to change them. Furthermore, since supply chains tend to be large in scale and complex in nature, supply chain strategies tend to be neither simple nor easy to comprehend, and we often have to make decisions based on incomplete, inexact and even incorrect information.

☙

Since rethinking a supply chain strategy is a *complex problem*, in order to tackle it we must learn how to deal with complexity.

Complexity: Objective vs. Subjective

In order to better deal with complexity, we must distinguish between two types of complexity: *objective* and *subjective*. To illustrate the difference between the two, let's use an example from everyday life: a game of chess.

Imagine a chess master pondering her next move. In front of her is a board where the first moves have led to the Sicilian Najdorf. The Najdorf is widely regarded as one of the most complex openings in all of chess, because it can transpose into many other, wildly different systems. The intrinsic complexity of this chess position is what we would call **objective** complexity: it is inherent to the problem itself, and is proportional to the number of elements in the system, the number of their possible states, and the number of relationships between elements and states. Objective complexity is *absolute*: it is independent of who is addressing the problem.

Now, imagine that our chess master looks to the adversary sitting in front of her. She knows this adversary from previous games: a young rookie from the local chess club, not particularly good in the Sicilian and with a reputation for making blunders under time pressure. "I can beat him easily," she thinks. Then our chess master looks at the chess clock ticking next to the board: she has more time left in the clock than her opponent has, and thinks: "I also have a time advantage." The relative complexity that the same chess position presents to each of the players, given their respective level of skill and the time they have left in the clock is what we would call **subjective** complexity. It depends on the objective complexity of the problem, for sure, but not exclusively. It also depends on the capacity of the person tackling the problem, by their ability to understand the system, and by the time pressure exerted upon them to make decisions and find a solution. Subjective complexity is relative: it depends on the problem **and** on who is addressing the problem.

Objective and subjective complexity are different in nature. The things we do in order to overcome them – or *tame* them – are also different.

Prescriptions to tame complexity

When it comes to dealing with complexity, there are bad news and good news. The bad news is that we can't eliminate complexity. It is a fact of life and we have to learn to live with it. The good news is that, even though complexity cannot be eliminated, we can learn to tame it. We may even use it to our advantage: chess world champions Bobby Fischer and Gary Kasparov were assiduous players of the Sicilian Najdorf.

Complexity is like a lion: it will *always* be a wild animal, but it can be taught some manners and even be turned into an ally. [*Competitive Advantage*] Below we present seven prescriptions that will help you tame complexity, to render it manageable.

The first three will help you reduce subjective complexity:
- *Rx #1:* Reduce the objective complexity of the system.
- *Rx #2:* Increase your ability to understand the system.
- *Rx #3:* Reduce time pressure in decision making.

The next four prescriptions will help you define the problem better.
- *Rx #4:* Clearly specify the desired end state.
- *Rx #5:* Tend to conflicts between partial goals.
- *Rx #6:* Increase your knowledge about the structure of the system.
- *Rx #7:* Get more complete information about the system.

By the time you are done reading this text, you will have received guidance regarding how to apply each one of these seven prescriptions to deal with the complexity of rethinking your supply chain strategy.

CHAPTER 2

our approach to the problem

Having described in broad terms the nature of the problem of rethinking a supply chain strategy, we now move to outlining the ideas that drive our approach to tackling it. An easy way to outline our approach is by pointing out the key ideas that we reject and the key ideas that we embrace. As a whole, this is what we call our *philosophy*.

Type-based vs Specific

We reject the idea that supply chain strategies can be described by means of *types*. For the last fifteen years, most research into supply chain strategies has been conducted based on the assumption that it makes sense to describe supply chain strategies using a limited number of clear-cut types: a *responsive* supply chain strategy, an *efficient* supply chain strategy, etc. A multitude of claims have been made using type-based approaches. Fisher's (1997) two-by-two matrix, published in his famous HBR article, may be the most cited of these claims: that a responsive supply chain strategy is a good match for innovative products, whereas an efficient supply chain strategy is a good match for functional products.

Claims like these are very appealing: they are intuitive and easy to grasp. However, empirical studies conducted to test their validity have found that the reduction of supply chain strategies to a few mutually exclusive types is not realistic. Real supply chain strategies are richer, more nuanced and more complex than what a single type or label can express.

Our approach to supply chain strategy has a different take on the matter: we see each supply chain strategy as a complex, nuanced and distinct entity. Therefore, we strive to describe it and evaluate it in terms **specific** to its own features and context. Companies are so peculiar, their supply chains are so diverse, and their environments are so particular, that when it comes to discussing a supply chain strategy there is little value in talking in general terms. We believe it is better to discuss things in terms specific to each situation: e.g. whether a specific supply chain strategy can support a specific overall strategy within a specific environment. Such an approach takes more time and effort, but is more realistic and actionable, and therefore more valuable.

Best practices vs Tailored practices

When a given practice has produced good results in contexts A and B, there is a natural temptation to apply it also in context C. Practices that have produced good results in the past when applied by others are often called **best practices**. The implication is that, if you were to apply them now, you would also get good results. Because what's sauce for the goose is sauce for the gander. Right? Wrong. We take the idea of **best practices** with a big grain of salt, because we think the efficacy of a practice depends on a plethora of factors regarding the context in which the practice is applied.

Generalizing best practices, even within the same industry, is a perilous enterprise. Attention should be paid to the peculiarities of each organization, including its strategy, its culture and its environment. When it comes to supply chain strategizing, one size does not fit all. Instead of copying what others have done elsewhere, it makes more sense to tailor an organization's practices to its particular situation: its culture, its strategy, its environment. This is what we call **tailored practices**. The idea is not to ignore all the lessons of the past, reinvent everything from scratch: there is obvious value in learning from what others have done. But whatever lessons we learn from others should be tailored to suit our own particular situation.

External and Internal Wisdom

An additional and related distinction we want to make is that between what we call *external wisdom* and *internal wisdom*. **External wisdom** refers to claims to knowledge that has been derived outside of our organization from empirical studies or the expert opinion of respected practitioners. The following are examples of external wisdom:

- the claim that innovative products are better served by supply chains focused on responsiveness, instead of focused on efficiency.
- the claim that companies whose facilities are geographically closer to each other tend to perform better.
- the claim that a supply chain can be at the same time agile, adaptable and aligned, and that being so will result in better performance.

It would be foolish to ignore external wisdom: there is much we can learn from the experience of others, from their past successes and failures. However, it would also be foolish to accept claims from external wisdom without first asking what evidence is there to support the claims, under what circumstances would the claim hold true, and whether they apply to a particular case.

Internal wisdom refers to the knowledge that an organization can distill from its own experience, from bringing its own experts together and discussing, often with the help of neutral facilitators, the nature of the challenges and opportunities facing the organization and the relative merits of the options available.[2]

Our approach to supply chain strategy relies heavily on internal wisdom. Of course we advise that practitioners stay abreast of the latest findings in the field of supply chain management, so that they can learn from the external wisdom published by experts and researchers in the field. But most importantly, we advocate that organizations take advantage of their own internal wisdom at the time of rethinking their supply chain strategy.

---

[2] Another example of internal wisdom is the knowledge derived from the expert analysis of data from the organization, and from initiatives such as Six Sigma exercises.

Fundamental tasks

We have identified at least seven distinct, fundamental tasks that must take place in order to rethink the supply chain strategy of an organization. These tasks are outlined below, in a sequence that roughly follows the order in which they would be conducted.

Task #1: Scoping

The first of the fundamental tasks, **Scoping**, is about defining the boundaries of the supply chain whose strategy will be revised. These boundaries are drawn in terms of the things that make the problem difficult, what we call the *axes of complexity*. Examples are time horizon, geography, product types, supplier types, customer types, channels, etc.

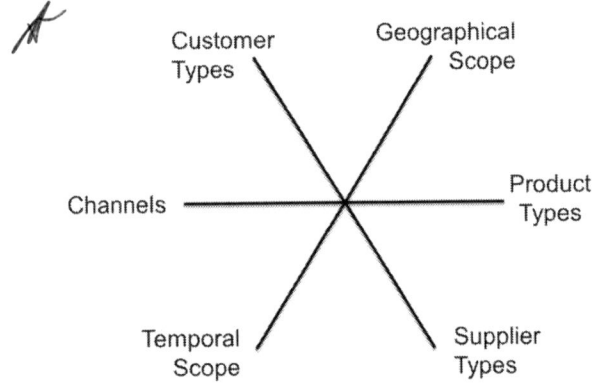

Figure 2: Examples of axes of complexity

Scoping, in short, is a balancing act along the axes of complexity.
- A *narrow* scope (i.e. focusing the strategizing exercise only on one product type, one customer type, one channel, one supplier type, a 1-year time horizon and a single geographical region) would be relatively easy to handle, but it would provide a rather poor representation of reality: it would be an oversimplification of a much richer problem.
- A *wide* scope (i.e. focusing the strategizing exercise on all product types, all customer types, all channels, all supplier types, a 50-year

time horizon and all geographical regions) would more accurately capture the richness of the real problem, but it would likely become intractable as a problem due to its complexity.
- A *good* scope will balance simplicity and realism, result in a challenging yet manageable exercise that is both realistic and tractable as a problem.

Let's see an example. Imagine that Coca-Cola wanted to rethink its supply chain strategy. The first task is to scope the problem. Including all of Coca-Cola's products sold through all of its channels, to all of its customers, from all of its suppliers, in the whole world and over a long time horizon, would make the problem very realistic but too complex to be manageable. Limiting the problem to the supply chain of the caramel flavoring used for caffeine-free diet Coke sold retail in convenience stores in the Boston area over a single year would make the problem too simplistic to be useful. A better scope would be to focus on the supply chain for carbonated beverages sold wholesale to the top three customer types in the New England area over a five-year period, including in the exercise only suppliers of strategic raw materials.

Task #2: Visioning

The second fundamental task, **Visioning**, is particularly relevant if the time horizon that was chosen through scoping is large enough to allow for dramatic changes to take place in the industry or the marketplace. If the time horizon chosen for the reformulation exercise is long relative to the *clockspeed*[3] of the industry where we operate, the future environment of the organization may be substantially different from the present environment of the organization. As time goes by, important changes may take place in the market, the industry and the world at large. We want our supply chain to be prepared for these changes. That is what visioning is about: envisioning the future environment of the organization where our supply chain may have to operate, so that we can anticipate its future challenges and opportunities.

---

[3] See Fine (1999).

Visioning reduces the likelihood that a future change will take you by surprise and require you to react in haste. One way to do Visioning for supply chain strategy is through scenarios, as described in Phadnis (2012).

Task #3: Specification

The third fundamental task, **Specification**, is about clearly stating the specific objectives that we expect our supply chain strategy to fulfill. Taken together, these objectives *specify* the desired outcome of our effort, and thus provide a *definition of success* for the supply chain strategy.

In defining specific objectives, one should be careful not to wade into dictating the *means* by which the objectives should be pursued. Specification is about stating the desired *ends*, not about prescribing the means that could be used to achieve them. Making an analogy with engineering, specification is equivalent to the definition of *'specs'* for a given product. The specifications do not tell you how to design the product down to the smallest details, but it tells you what expectations there are on the finished design. Specification defines success for you, but does not map your way to achieve it.

Specification should consider the output of the visioning task, since our definition of success in a given future will depend on what we anticipate the future will look like.

Task #4: Articulation

The fourth fundamental task, **Articulation**, is about expressing a given supply chain strategy in explicit terms. There are multiple supply chain strategies that may be articulated. For sure, we must articulate the current supply chain strategy of the organization. But articulation is not limited to *our current* supply chain strategy: we can also articulate the supply chain strategy of a competitor, or a new supply chain strategy that we are considering as an alternative to replace the one we have in place right now.

We have developed an approach to articulating a supply chain strategy as a conceptual system, that is to say, as a group of ideas working together towards common goals. Our proposed method for supply chain strategy articulation will be discussed in detail in Chapters 4 and 5.

Task #5: Evaluation

The fifth fundamental task, **Evaluation**, is about assessing to what extent a given supply chain strategy works towards achieving a desired set of objectives. This requires us to know both what supply chain strategy we are evaluating and what are the objectives that it should fulfill, which makes both Articulation and Specification prerequisites for Evaluation. In Chapters 6 and 7 we present and discuss a set of evaluation criteria that – in our view - any supply chain strategy, or functional strategy for that matter, should satisfy.

Task #6: Generation

The sixth fundamental task is the **Generation** of new ideas regarding what is possible in terms of the strategy. This is when we bring innovative and creative thinking into the process. The purpose of Generation is to innovate: to propose as many new good ideas as possible regarding how to improve our supply chain strategy. Creativity, not selectivity, is the goal here. Generation requires us to know what areas need to be improved upon, which makes Evaluation a prerequisite. It also requires us to know what objectives we are shooting for, which makes Specification a prerequisite.

Task #7: Selection

The seventh fundamental task is the **Selection** of the best ideas for our new supply chain strategy, from among all the possible good ideas generated in the previous task. This is when we bring rigorous and selective thinking into the process. The purpose of Selection is to retain as many good features of the existing supply chain strategy as possible, while replacing all the weak ones with new features, in a manner that is internally consistent and strategically aligned with the overall strategy. Since it builds upon each of the previous tasks, they are all prerequisites for Selection.

In our approach, *Generation* and *Selection* are conducted hand-in-hand. They are conducted using a systematic method for strategy elaboration, presented and discussed in Chapters 8 and 9.

After these seven tasks, we can proceed to the **Implementation** of the new supply chain strategy. Implementation is about translating the new supply chain strategy into action. Implementation is not in itself part of the process of *rethinking* the supply chain strategy and is therefore outside of the scope of this text.

The seven fundamental tasks we have outlined above are our answer to the three basic challenges that rethinking a supply chain strategy presents to practitioners, and – as we will argue at the end of the text – are in line with the seven prescriptions we issued to deal with its complexity.

CHAPTER 3

a framework for rethinking SCS

Before we can *rethink* a supply chain strategy, we need to learn how to *think* about it in the first place. Supply chain strategy is an abstract concept, whose definition can be the subject of endless academic discussion. We have little interest in such debates beyond what is necessary to have a grounded and useful conversation about the challenges that the subject presents to people like you: real supply chain managers.

A definition of supply chain strategy

Through a series of collaborative management research projects, we have developed and refined a pragmatic approach to rethinking a supply chain strategy. A key part of that approach is a working *definition* of what we mean when we talk about the *supply chain strategy* of an organization:

> *"The supply chain strategy of an organization can be defined as the collection of general and specific objectives, policies and choices made in a supply chain to align its operations with the overall strategy of the organization."*

This definition has proven a useful foundation to our efforts.

Strategizing in multiple dimensions

Thinking about a supply chain strategy requires us to think along multiple dimensions.

Supply-demand The first dimension is the most familiar: it runs from supplier to consumer, and back. The concept of a *supply chain* (or *demand chain*, as it has also been called) immediately invites us to think along the *supply-demand* dimension. The overall objective of a supply chain strategy along this dimension is to successfully match demand and supply.

Thematic range A second dimension cuts across all the supply-chain relevant[4] functions of the organization, along what we call the *thematic range*. The overall objective of a supply chain strategy along this dimension is to harmonize the efforts of all the supply-chain relevant functions towards the fulfillment of the overall strategy.

Strategy-operations The third dimension we must consider runs from the top down, from the overall strategy of the organization to its operations in the supply chain, along what we call the *strategy-operations continuum*. The overall objective of a supply chain strategy along this dimension is to serve as a logical bridge between the overall strategy of an organization and its operational practices in the supply chain.

Around these three dimensions, we have developed a working model of a supply chain strategy, which has been tested and revised through multiple collaborative management research projects. It includes both the supply chain strategy of an organization *and* the context where it operates, and serves as a common platform to connect the diverse techniques used in our approach, which will be discussed in Chapters 4 through 9.

The logic and elements of this working model are explained below.

Bridging the gap

As we stated before, the supply chain strategy serves as the logical bridge between the overall strategy of an organization and the operational practices of its supply chain. To understand how this bridging occurs, it is

---

[4] The term "supply-chain relevant" – which we will use frequently and will abbreviate as SCR – refers to anything that has an effect on the supply chain of the organization, irrespective of whether it falls under the jurisdiction of the organization's supply chain *function*. Thus, for example, policies regarding forecasting, procurement, production and sales are clearly *supply-chain relevant*, even though they often are outside the jurisdiction of the supply chain function.

useful to think of the overall strategy and the operational practices as found at opposite ends of the strategy-operations continuum, with a gap between them (Figure 3.)

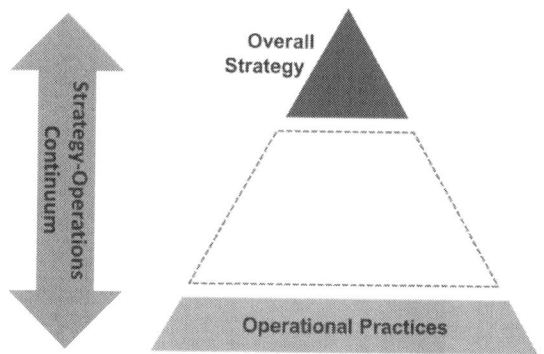

Figure 3: Gap between strategy and operations

The **overall strategy** – found near the top of the continuum – is composed of concepts that are more *strategic* in focus, more *abstract* in nature, *wider* in scope and mostly about *purpose* (Figure 4.)

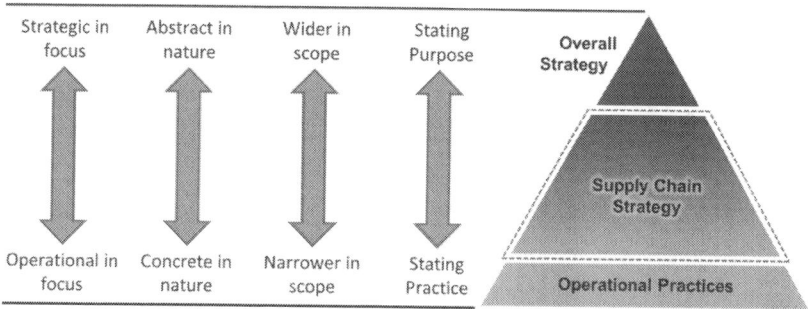

Figure 4: Supply chain strategy as a bridge across the gap

The **operational practices** – found near the bottom of the continuum – are composed of concepts that are more *operational* in focus, more *concrete* in nature, *narrower* in scope and mostly about *practice*.

Bridging the gap between the two along the continuum is the **supply chain strategy**. The supply chain strategy is composed of concepts that are more operational than those in the overall strategy, yet more strategic than those in the operational practices; more concrete than those in the overall strategy, yet more abstract than those in the operational practices; narrower in scope than those in the overall strategy, yet wider in scope than those in the operational practices; and more about practice than those in the overall strategy, yet more about purpose than those in the operational practices.

Adding granularity

So far we have talked about the overall strategy and the supply chain strategy as single entities. Let us now add granularity by slicing them into finer elements along the strategy-operations continuum.[5]

Figure 5: An organization strategy decomposed into elements

A typical overall strategy can be articulated in the form of a short mission statement, which we call the strategy **Core**, and a set of three to five general statements of purpose, which we call the strategy **Pillars**. These two layers of elements, the Core and the Pillars, are easily found explicitly stated in most overall strategies. (In Figure 5 and subsequent figures, the letter C refers to the Core.)

The supply chain strategy, in turn, can also be sliced into finer layers of elements along the continuum, as shown in Figure 6: general objectives for the supply chain (which we call **Principles**), specific objectives for the supply chain (which we call **Imperatives**), and specific decisions made to support these objectives (which we call **Policies and Choices**.) The Policies and Choices are then finally implemented in the form of **Operational Practices** throughout the supply chain of the organization. These lie at the

---

[5] In our experience, these divisions into *layers* or *levels* along the strategy operations continuum, albeit somewhat arbitrary, are very useful.

lower end of the strategy operations-continuum.

Figure 6: A supply chain strategy decomposed into elements

The conceptual elements

The six layers of concepts we have introduced above, from the Core to the Practices (see Figure 7), are what we call the **conceptual elements**, because for the purposes of supply chain strategizing, we consider them mostly as ideas, or *concepts*, that can be rethought.

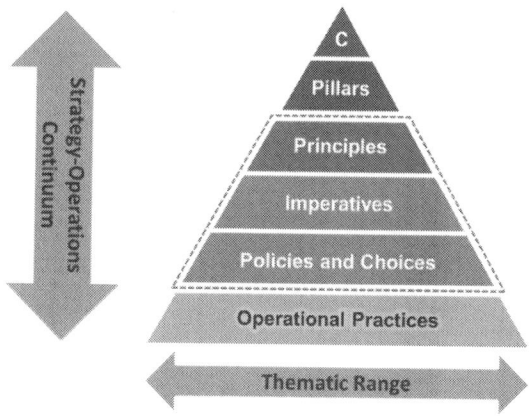

Figure 7: The six layers of conceptual elements

As shown in Figure 7, these layers of concepts follow a logical sequence along the strategy-operations continuum, from the strategy core to the operational practices. The layers demarcated by the dotted polygon, namely the Principles, Imperatives, Policies and Choices, when taken as a whole, are what we call the supply chain strategy of an organization.

The number of concepts multiplies as we move down the layers.
- Although there is typically only one **Core**, there are usually

around three to five **Pillars** supporting it.
- There are usually two to four times as many **Principles** as there are Pillars.
- Each Principle has under it between two and four **Imperatives**.
- Each Imperative will have under it between two to four **Policies and Choices**.

As they multiply, concepts also become more specific and concrete, covering a wider range of supply-chain relevant themes, including multiple areas of interest and activity for the supply chain. This fanning out of the ideas, which give the conceptual elements its characteristic pyramidal form, is what we call the **Thematic Range**.

The enabling elements

Providing a context to the conceptual elements we have the supply-chain relevant assets, culture and capabilities of the organization:

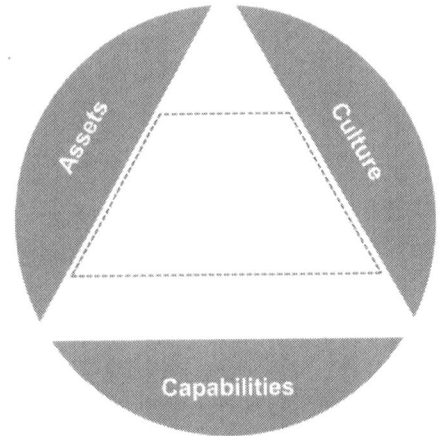

Figure 8: The enabling elements: assets, culture and capabilities

- **Assets** *are the things we have to do work with.* Assets can be material, human, financial, etc.
- **Culture** *is the way we do things.* Culture affects decisions, behaviors, and – consequently – results.
- **Capabilities** *are the things we know how to do.* Capabilities refer to

the ability to do a task.

Since their role is to enable and support the supply chain strategy, we call these the 'enabling elements' (Figure 8.) In the long run, the enabling elements should adapt to the supply chain strategy, and *not* the other way around. One thing the enabling elements have in common is that it takes time to change them: they have more *inertia* than the conceptual elements. This is why sometimes we refer to these as inertial elements.

The internal elements

Something the conceptual elements and the enabling elements have in common is that they all are within the control of the organization.

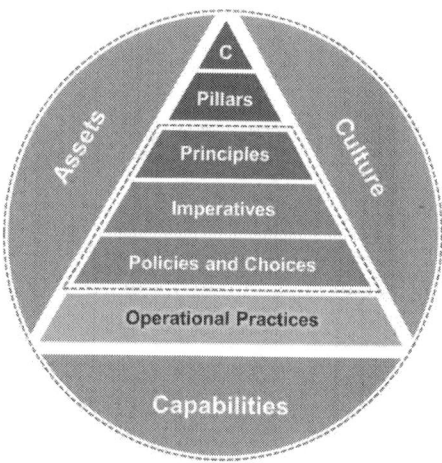

Figure 9: The internal elements: what the organization controls

In other words, the organization can change at will its overall and supply chain strategies and practices, and – with time- its assets, culture and capabilities. That is why, together, we refer to these elements as the **internal elements**. The dotted circumference in Figure 9 indicates what falls within the control of the organization.

The external elements

Many other things that matter for rethinking the supply chain strategy of an organization fall beyond its control. We refer to these as **external elements**. In our model, they are represented outside the dotted circumference.

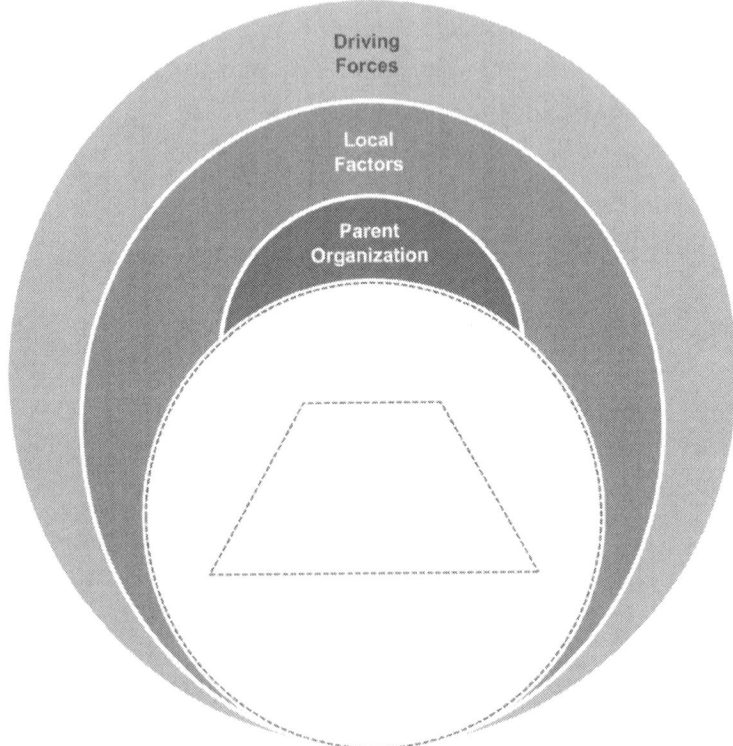

Figure 10: The external elements: beyond the organization's control

As shown in Figure 10, we identify three types of external elements that should be considered when rethinking the supply chain strategy. The most immediate of the external elements are the guidelines and expectations of a ***parent organization***, if there is one. Not all organizations happen to belong to a parent organization. But many do. For example:

- ChemCo's Specialty Pigments business unit, when rethinking its supply chain strategy, must consider the corporate expectations of its parent organization, ChemCo Corporation. This includes ChemCo's corporate-level strategy, values, policies and guidelines. Even though

they may be *influenced*, these corporate expectations are not *controlled* by the Specialty Pigments business unit itself. Thus, they are considered external for strategizing purposes.
- The United Nations (UN) Peacekeeping's Department of Field Support (DFS), when rethinking its supply chain strategy, must consider the expectations of its parent organization, the United Nations: its values, policies, guidelines, etc. Since the expectations of the UN are not controlled by DFS, they should be considered external to DFS.

Beyond the realm of the parent organization, lies a multitude of variables that have a significant effect on the organization and its supply chain, and that are also beyond its control. Following the advice of Phadnis (2012), we classify these variables based on whether the organization can have any *influence* on them, as follows:
- The variables that are beyond control, but *not beyond the influence*, of the organization, are called **local factors**. In the case of an organization unit, local factors refer mostly to variables from the market and industry where the business unit operates. These can be influenced by the business unit.
- The variables that are beyond both the control *and* the influence of the organization, and still have a significant effect on the organization and its supply chain, are called **driving forces**. These come from the surrounding environment and the world at large, and include things like demographics, geography, climate change, etc.

The complete picture

When we combine the external and the internal elements, the complete picture of our working model emerges. It is shown in Figure 11. The supply chain strategy – demarcated by the dotted polygon – lies at the center of the conceptual elements, bridging the overall strategy and the supply chain operations. Around them are the enabling elements: assets, culture and capabilities. All these internal elements fall inside the dotted circumference, because they are within our control. Beyond our control are the external elements: the expectations of the parent organization, the local factors and the driving forces.

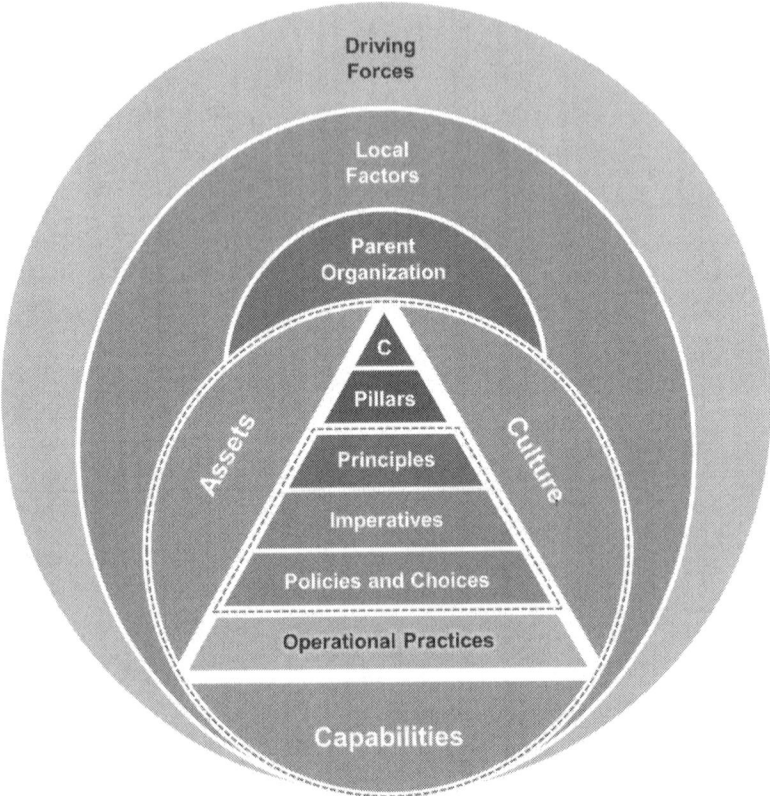

Figure 11: A working model for rethinking a supply chain strategy

This working model, as presented above, provides a structure to our approach to rethinking the supply chain strategy of an organization, and will be used as a reference throughout the rest of this text.

CHAPTER 4

capturing your SCS

Back in Chapter 1, we listed three distinct basic challenges that we believe you will face if you want to rethink your supply chain strategy, regardless of what approach you follow. The first one of these challenges – and possibly the most neglected one – is to assess your current supply chain strategy. Understanding what you have in place today is fundamental, since it is the starting point for all subsequent improvement efforts.

Later in Chapter 2 we listed several fundamental tasks that are part of rethinking the supply chain strategy of an organization. One of these tasks, which we called **Articulation**, is about expressing a given supply chain strategy in explicit terms. As part of the MIT Supply Chain 2020 Project, we have developed an approach to articulate the current supply chain strategy of an organization.

In this chapter we present this approach and the key ideas behind it.

Categorization vs Articulation

You may recall from Chapter 1 that we consider supply chain strategies rich, nuanced and complex entities, which cannot be accurately characterized by means of a few simple *types*. Unfortunately, most scholarship on the subject of supply chain strategy relies heavily on the use of types for characterization – an approach that we call *categorization*. Examples of categorization of supply chain strategies over the last fifteen years are plentiful, from Fisher's (1997) two types, to Lee's (2002) four types to Perez's (2013) six types.

We reject *categorization* as a useful approach to characterize the supply chain strategy of an organization, on two accounts. The first is that it is not clear how valid these types – and the claims associated with them – are. The second is that – based on our own experience with rethinking supply chain strategies – supply chains are so peculiar and their contexts so diverse, that discussing a supply chain strategy in terms of a few general types grossly underestimates the complexity of the subject.

Instead, we strive to describe each supply chain strategy in terms of its own particular features – an approach we call *articulation*. Articulation is to categorization what a charcoal portrait is to a smiley icon. Whereas categorization simplifies the features in order to find commonality, articulation seeks to represent each feature with sufficient detail. It follows that articulation takes much more time and effort than categorization, but it is also much more realistic, and – as we will see in later chapters – much more useful a starting point for evaluation and reformulation.

Just as there are many ways to 'capture' a human face (i.e. a photo, a pencil sketch, an oil portrait, an X-ray of the skull, etc.), there may be many ways to characterize and articulate a supply chain strategy. Our approach is to characterize the supply chain strategy of an organization as a conceptual system, that is to say, as a group of interrelated ideas working together to achieve common goals. We then articulate this conceptual system by means of a conceptual map, that is to say, as a depiction of interrelated ideas.

This may sound complicated now, but rest assured that the basic idea is very simple and powerful. Making a conceptual map – albeit time-consuming – is not a difficult task, as will be shown in the following pages.

Mapping concepts 101

What follows is a simple example of how to make a small conceptual map, based on a 2005 case study about Dell's supply chain[6]. Consider the following passage:

> *In many cases Dell directly deals with tier-2 suppliers. Dell negotiates on behalf of its tier-1 suppliers to aggregate volume and leverage its own buying power. Dell's main objective in doing so is to ensure continuity of supply and reduce procurement costs further.*

Let's start with the first sentence and a half. From it, the following idea is evident: *Negotiate directly with tier-2 suppliers on behalf of tier-1 suppliers.* Notice we have reworded it to start with a verb, so it suggests an action or purpose. Let's put that idea inside a box (see Figure 12).

> Negotiate directly with tier-2 suppliers on behalf of tier-1 suppliers.

Figure 12: An idea inside a box

Once an idea has been worded to start with a verb, and framed inside a box, it has become what we call a **Concept**. Concepts like these are the blocks for building conceptual maps that will allow us to articulate our supply chain strategy.

Let's keep reading the passage above to identify additional *concepts*. The second half of the second sentence yields these two ideas: *Aggregate volume in procurement orders* and *Leverage Dell's buying power*. Notice we reworded a bit where clarity required it. We box them (see Figure 13).

> Aggregate volume of procurement orders

> Leverage Dell's buying power

Figure 13: Two additional concepts

---

[6] Taken from section 5.2.1.2 of S. Roy (2005). The 2nd and 3rd sentences were swapped. We use these passages as an example, and make no claim as to their veracity.

Based on the passage, there is a relationship between the first idea and the two new ones: the former is done in order to achieve the latter. Let's use *lines* to indicate a purposeful link between concepts. Let's also arrange the concepts vertically so that those beneath are done with the purpose of supporting those above them. Then, the three concepts – and the relationship of purpose among them – would be represented as shown below:

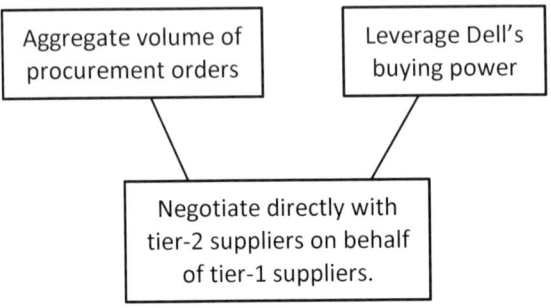

Figure 14: A tiny conceptual map

Look at Figure 14. It's simple, right? Well, these three boxes with text and two lines connecting them actually constitute a (very small) **conceptual map**, that is to say, a map of ideas and the relationships of purpose between them.

If you look at the map in Figure 14 from the top down, you will notice it has two *levels*: on the higher level, the one near the top of the page, there are two concepts, while on the lower level, the one near the bottom of the page, there is one concept. Maps don't have to be limited to two levels, though. As we add new concepts, they may fall into higher or lower levels. Given any concept, there is a surefire way to add concepts to the level **beneath** it: all we have to do is ask "***How?***" as in *How is this achieved?* For example: given the concept *"Leverage Dell's buying power"*, if we want to add concepts to a level beneath it, all we have to do is answer the question "How?" e.g. how is this buying power leveraged?

Likewise, given any concept, there is a surefire way to add concepts to the level **above** it: all we have to do is ask "***Why?***" as in *Why do we want to do this?* For example, given the concept *"Leverage Dell's buying power"*, if we want to add concepts to a level above it, all we have to do is answer the question "Why?" e.g. why do we want to leverage Dell's buying power? The answer, as seen in the last sentence of the passage from the case, is twofold: we do so, because we want to *Ensure continuity of supply* and *Reduce procurement costs further*. We can add these two concepts to the map, in a new level, as shown in Figure 15 below.

```
                    ┌──────────────────┐    ┌──────────────────┐
This                │ Ensure continuity│    │ Reduce procurement│
way to              │    of supply     │    │   costs further   │
"Why?"              └──────────────────┘    └──────────────────┘

        ┌──────────────────────┐      ┌──────────────────┐
        │  Aggregate volume of │      │  Leverage Dell's │
        │  procurement orders  │      │   buying power   │
        └──────────────────────┘      └──────────────────┘

This                ┌──────────────────────────┐
way to              │  Negotiate directly with │
"How?"              │ tier-2 suppliers on behalf│
                    │    of tier-1 suppliers.   │
                    └──────────────────────────┘
```

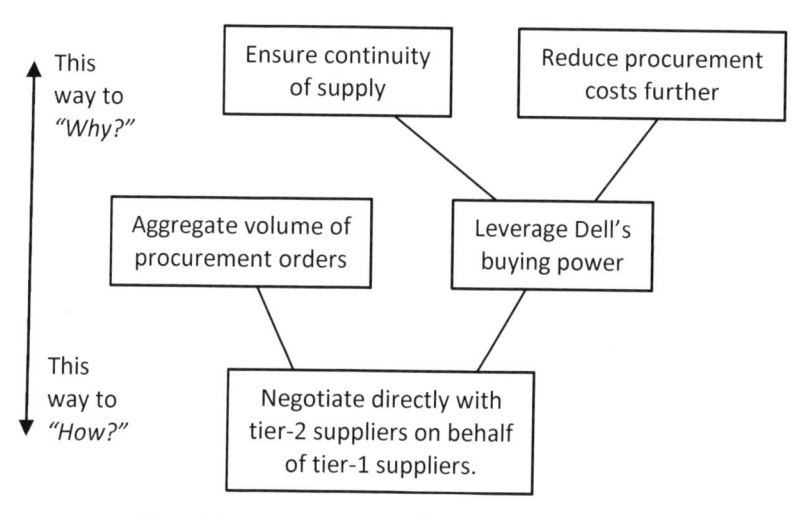

Figure 15: Our conceptual map has a new level on top

Now let's talk about how to read a conceptual map, with an example. Take one concept from Figure 15, *"Leverage Dell's buying power"* for example, and use it as your starting point. You will see in the map that other concepts are connected to it through lines. This is because these other concepts are deemed to be related to it:

- Linked concepts above it are the answer the question *"Why?"*, thus providing a reason for it, a purpose. For example, one reason to *leverage Dell's buying power* is to *reduce procurement costs further*.
- Linked concepts beneath it are the answer to the question *"How?"*, thus providing a means or ways to achieve it. For example, a way to *leverage Dell's buying power* is to *negotiate directly with tier-2 suppliers on behalf of tier-1 suppliers.*

After this short map reading exercise, you can appreciate the advantage of wording the concepts in a short, concise way and starting with a verb.

Even though the conceptual map we just made is a small one, the simple steps we followed to make it are the same steps that are used to make much larger conceptual maps, the kind that are required to articulate an entire supply chain strategy. At the risk of oversimplification, the steps can be stated thus:

1. Identify the concepts and word them clearly.
2. Identify *why* and *how* relationships between concepts.
3. Display the concepts and their relationships graphically.

More information on how to make a map is provided later.

Vertical axis: the strategy-operations continuum

Take a look at Figure 15. What does it mean for a concept to be higher or lower along the vertical axis? The higher a concept is along the vertical axis, the more it is about *why* we do things, that is to say, the more it is a statement of purpose. The lower a concept is along the vertical axis, the more it is about *how* we do things, that is to say, the more it is a statement of practice.

We call this vertical axis the **strategy-operations continuum**, which we introduced back in Chapter 3. As indicated in Figure 4, concepts higher in the continuum are more strategic in focus, more abstract in nature, and wider in scope; whereas concepts lower in the continuum are more operational in focus, more concrete in nature, and narrower in scope. Now, after building your first conceptual map, you can see the reason for this: the higher a concept lies in the vertical axis, the more it is about *why*, about purpose, about the overall **strategy**; and – by the same token – the lower it is in the vertical axis, the more it is about *how*, about practice, about the supply chain **operations**.

You may notice, for example in Figure 7, our working model for rethinking a supply chain strategy distinguishes six levels of conceptual elements along the vertical axis. These discrete layers will be very handy to *craft* a *new* supply chain strategy, as you will see in Chapter 8. However, the fact remains that they are somewhat arbitrary. Thus, when the objective is to *capture* your *current* supply chain strategy by building a conceptual map, I invite you to think about the vertical axis not as sequence of discrete levels but instead as a **continuum**. When you are building a conceptual map, place each concept vertically where you feel it belong, based on its *how* and *why* relationship with other concepts. Until the map is populated, do not worry about assigning them to specific layers of *Principles, Imperatives*, and *Policies and Choices*.

Horizontal axis: the thematic range

The small conceptual map shown in Figure 15 was built based on a single short passage from a case study about Dell. The theme of that passage was – broadly speaking –procurement. The case study we used as source, Roy (2005), has more to say about Dell's approach to procurement, but it also has more to say about other supply-chain relevant topics besides procurement, such as inventory, assembly, sales, etc. If we were to continue mapping these other passages of the case study, we would end up with a much wider conceptual map that would address a multitude of subjects, not only procurement. Consider Figure 16, a conceptual map prepared back in 2007– using precisely Roy's (2005) case study on Dell as a source. Admittedly, this map is rather rudimentary: it was done as homework for a doctoral class, with the sole purpose of exploring the feasibility of using a conceptual map to articulate a supply chain strategy.

By reading the concepts in the map of Figure 16 from left to right (or right to left – it doesn't matter, as long as it is horizontally), you will clearly sense that a variety of themes are addressed: inbound transportation, centralization of operations, incentives for suppliers, workforce flexibility, inventory visibility, are – among many others – supply-chain relevant subjects that are covered in this specific conceptual map.

Since the supply chain of an organization is by definition a cross-functional entity, it follows that – when capturing a supply chain strategy – we will discuss a wide **range** of supply-chain relevant **themes**, from suppliers to customers, from planning to fulfillment, from inventory to service, from cost to innovation. In the conceptual map, this diversity of subjects is reflected along the horizontal axis, in the form of what we call the ***thematic range*** of the conceptual map, an idea we presented back in Chapter 3 and illustrated in Figure 7. As we will see in Chapter 6 when we discuss the criteria of *coverage*, finding omissions in the thematic range of a well-done conceptual map is a sign of blind-spots in a supply chain strategy.

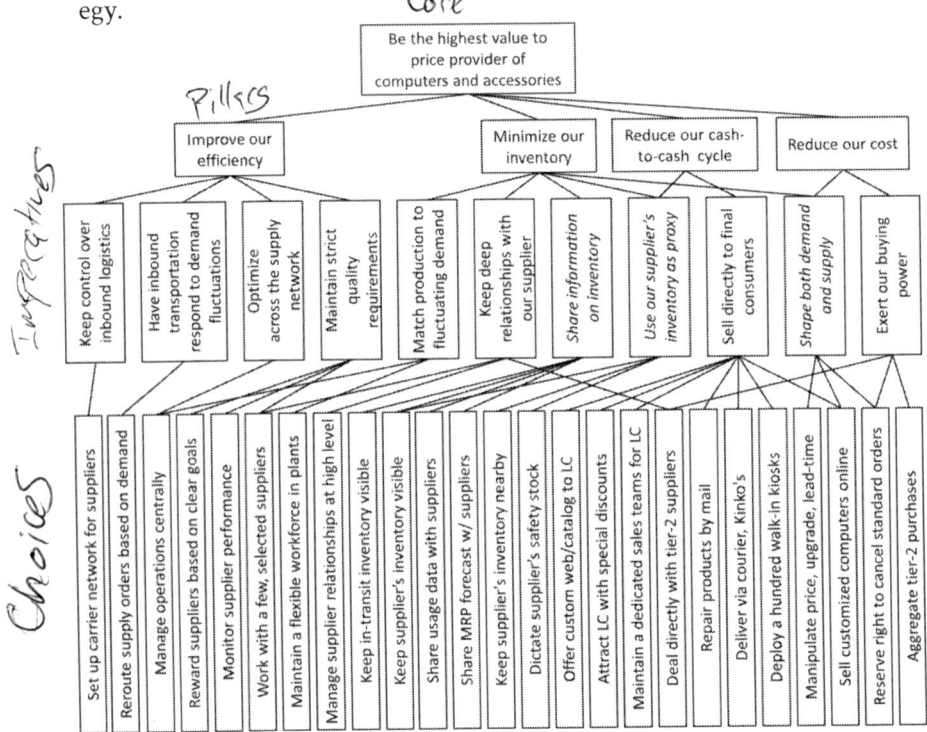

Figure 16: A conceptual map based on Roy's (2005) case on Dell

Now that we have discussed the vertical and horizontal axes, we can rewrite the broad steps to build a conceptual map, as follows:

1. Identify the concepts. Make sure to word them clearly and concisely, starting with a verb, and put them inside boxes.
2. Arrange the concepts horizontally according to subject, across the

thematic range.
3. Identify the *why* and *how* relationships between concepts, and represent them graphically as lines connecting the boxes.
4. Sort the concepts vertically using the logic of the strategy-operations continuum.

When mapping, hold judgment

When a team from an organization sets out to map their current supply chain strategy, it should stay focused on the task at hand: *mapping* the practices and purposes of the supply chain – warts and all – along the strategy-operations continuum and the thematic range. The temptation to start *evaluating* the results of the current strategy on the fly will be strong, but it should be resisted: *articulation* is about capturing the practices of the supply chain and the purposes behind them, not judging the results of these practices. All judgment about the outcome of the strategy should be noted and put aside until the evaluation stage.

It is important to point this out because, since companies usually do not articulate the current state of things, as soon as the map of the current strategy starts to emerge, some members will be eager to have the record reflect that some things went wrong with the strategy. Let me illustrate this with a real example, taken from one of our projects.

> *The company decided to centralize their customer service operations, with the purpose of improving the quality of their service. However, the centralization of the operations actually resulted in a deterioration of the quality of customer service, the opposite of what was intended.*

As we articulate the current supply chain strategy of an organization, it is paramount to stay focused on capturing practices and their purposes. In the example above, for example, we can identify this factual concept of practice: "Centralize the customer service operations."

42 | MIT SCS LAB

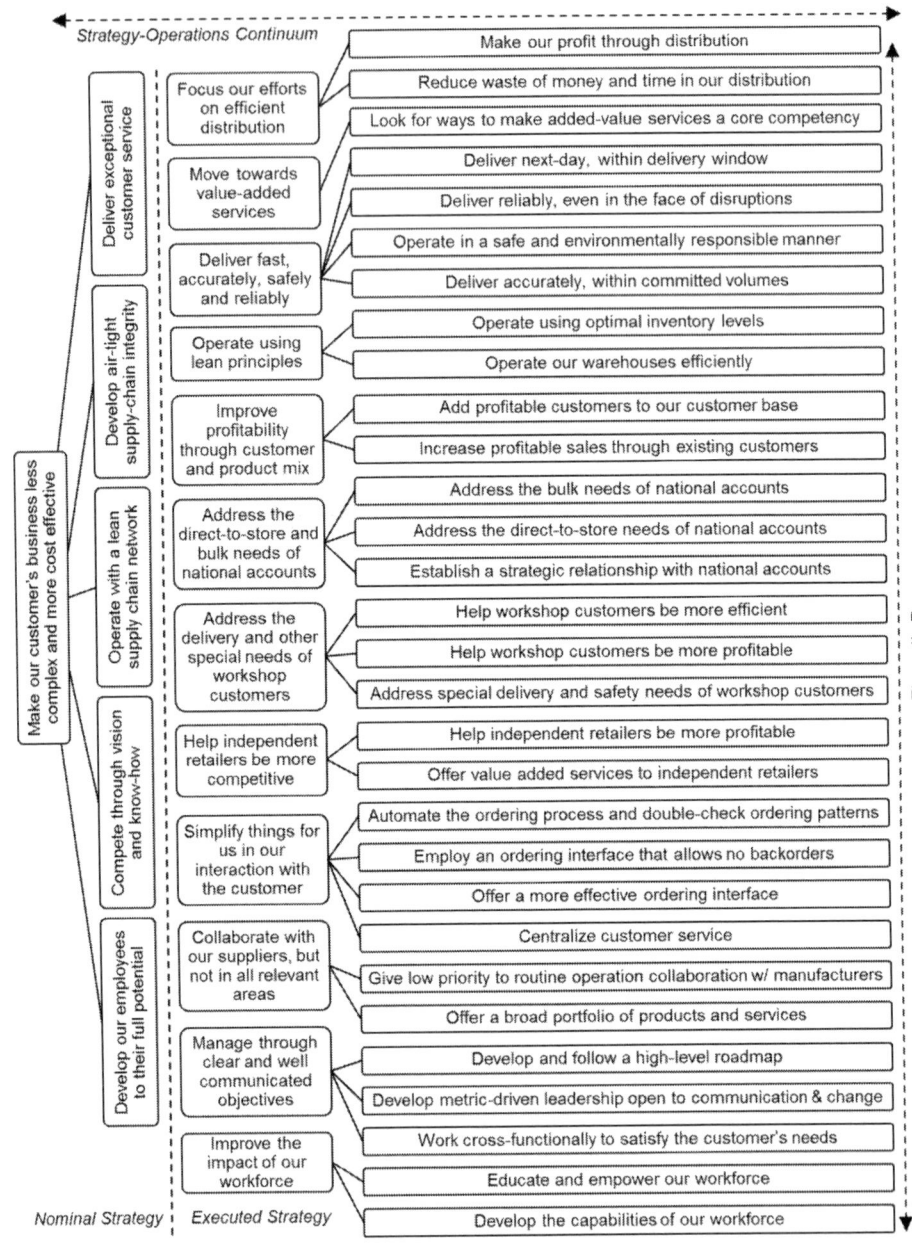

Figure 17: Conceptual map of Libica's supply chain strategy

Likewise, we can identify a concept from the reason this was done (its *Why?*): "Improve the quality of service." The fact that the decision backfired is not part of the strategy, but a result of it, so they are not part of articulation. If the comment is made, we make a note and then put it aside until the evaluation.

Nominal and Executed

It is useful to differentiate between high-level strategic statements, which we call the ***nominal strategy***, and mid-level statements of practice and purpose, which we call the ***executed strategy***. A useful approach to building a map of the current supply chain strategy of an organization is to map the nominal strategy from the ***top-down***, and to map the executed strategy from the ***bottom-up***.

Let's see an example. Figure 17 shows a conceptual map that articulates the current supply chain strategy (as of 2009) of a company we will call Libica. So that it would fit in the page, the map has been rotated. This conceptual map was done by mapping Libica's nominal strategy from the top down, and Libica's executed strategy from the bottom up. What follows is a description of this process.

The nominal strategy

Libica's *nominal strategy* was mapped from the ***top-down***, based on information provided to us by their Senior VP of Supply Chain. Libica's strategy ***Core***, the single statement that captures the gist of its strategic mission, is: "*Make our customer's business less complex and more cost effective.*" The core is placed as a concept right on top, at the high end of the strategy-operations continuum. Then come Libica's strategy ***Pillars***, the general statements of purpose that answer the question: 'How will we achieve the core?' As shown in Figure 17, there are five pillars in Libica's nominal strategy:

- *Deliver exceptional customer service.*
- *Develop air-tight supply-chain integrity.*

- *Operate with a lean supply chain network.*
- *Compete through vision and know-how.*
- *Develop our employees to their full potential.*

These concepts are boxed and placed right beneath the strategy core concept. This is shown on the left side of Figure 17.

The executed strategy

Libica's *executed strategy* was mapped from the **bottom-up**, based on information collected in twenty interviews with different VPs and Directors from supply-chain related functions within Libica. The one-on-one interviews, each about an hour long and conducted over the phone, sought to identify Libica's actual practices, policies and choices in the most prominent supply-chain related areas, and to identify the underlying ideas behind them. For each supply chain practice we identified, we asked 'Why do you do this? What is the purpose?" This allowed us to identify new concepts higher in the strategy-operations continuum. We asked 'Why?' several times for each concept. The resulting map is shown on the right side of Figure 17.

The final conceptual map

At the end, we had two half-maps: one for the *nominal strategy* and the one for the *executed strategy*. Following the logic of the strategy-operations continuum, we placed the nominal strategy map on top of the executed strategy map. The resulting conceptual map, showing only the topmost four conceptual levels - and rotated for the sake of printing space - is shown in Figure 17.

You may remember the working model we presented before. If you don't, take another look at Figure 11. The four levels shown in the conceptual map of Figure 17 correspond to the top four levels of conceptual elements in our working model. To help you visualize this correspondence, see Figure 18, where we have rotated the model's levels accordingly. The reason only four levels are shown in the map in Figure 17 is because the other levels, the ones not shown, include so many concepts that they would require a larger paper size.

A clear and factual articulation of the supply chain strategy of an organization, which is what the conceptual map of Figure 17 is, can be very useful as a starting point for its evaluation and reformulating, as we will discuss in Chapters 6 and 8, respectively.

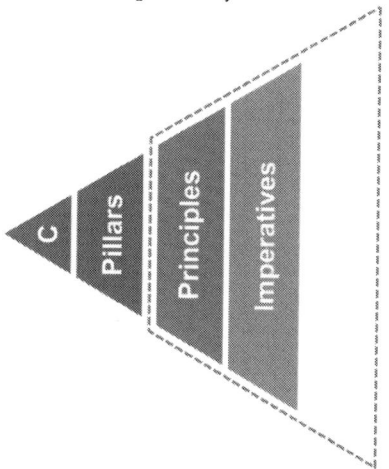

Figure 18: The four levels of the previous FSM, in the model

More details regarding how Libica's conceptual map was developed – in case you are curious – are presented in the next chapter, along with a detailed protocol to capture the supply chain strategy of an organization.

CHAPTER 5

a protocol for capture

What follows is a detailed, actionable protocol – written with managers like you in mind - presenting our method to capture the supply chain strategy of an organization and to express it in the form of a conceptual map. Unless you are planning to apply this protocol soon, you can skip this chapter and come back to them when needed.

We call it the Functional Strategy Mapping Method, which we abbreviate as *FSM Method*. We refer to the resulting map as a *Functional Strategy Map*, which we abbreviate as FSM. We divide the protocol for the FSM Method into ten steps. Each step is illustrated with examples.

Step 1 - Scope

The first step is to define the scope of the mapping exercise, by identifying and listing the relevant **Areas** of the organization and its supply chain to be included. Will we include sales and marketing? Will we include procurement? Manufacturing? Finance? The resulting short-list of relevant functional areas is not meant to be final: we should remain open to adding new areas as needed during the course of the project.

Once the list of relevant areas is prepared, the facilitator proceeds to identify individuals within these areas to be interviewed. For each area, there are three levels of the organizational hierarchy from which respondents should be chosen in roughly equal numbers:

1. **Level 1** is composed of individuals at the lowest hierarchical level *directly* involved with the process of crafting the overall strategy of the organization. These are people that have a say in the overall strategy.
2. **Level 2** is composed of individuals that report directly to Level 1 individuals. By definition, they do not participate directly in crafting the overall strategy, although they might provide input indirectly.
3. **Level 3** is composed of individuals that report to Level 2 individuals.

The initial selection of respondents is not final: the facilitator should allow for *'snowball sampling'*, e.g. should be willing to add new respondents on the go, based on what is being heard in the interviews.

Example

A $100B company that we will call Libica[7] approached CTL. Its business model had just been modified to better fit its evolving marketplace. The Executive Vice President of Operations of Libica decided to ask for our help in rethinking their supply chain strategy.

To capture their supply chain strategy, it was decided that the project would focus on the Distribution business unit of Libica. Areas that were deemed relevant to the supply chain included operations, marketing, sales, strategy, procurement, and customer service. The list of respondents is shown in Table 1.

Step 2 - Conduct qualitative interviews

The second step is to conduct a series of interviews with these respondents, with the purpose of finding out about the tacit supply chain strategy of the organization, via their supply chain activities. For obvious reasons, the questions during these interviews cannot be posed in these terms. Instead we ask about the *activities* that *individuals* perform.

The individual serves as a proxy to tap into the organization. Similarly, the specific activities serve as proxy to the tacit knowledge of the supply chain strategy, as reflected in its objectives, policies and choices. This

---

[7] All sensitive information has been duly disguised.

means that, even though the interviews start by asking about the activities of an individual, the conversation should be steered as soon as possible towards the objectives, policies and choices of the supply chain, as reflected in these activities.

Level 1 *(7 individuals)*
Executive VP of Strategic Sourcing
Senior VP of Marketing and Retail Sales
Senior VP of Operational Excellence
Senior VP of Customer Service
Senior VP of Strategy and Business Development
Executive VP of Operations and Supply Chain
Senior VP of National Chain Accounts

Level 2 *(7 individuals)*
VP of Operations - West Region
VP of Operations - East Region
VP of Operations - Central Region
VP of Specialty Sales
VP of Information Technology
VP of Strategic Planning and Execution
VP of Operational Excellence

Level 3 *(8 individuals)*
Director of Inventory Optimization
Director of Operations (x2)
Director of Retail Sales (x2)
Director of Consumer Products
Manager of Performance Cons.
Director of Marketing & Product Development

Table 1: List of respondents from Libica

The interviews required by the FSM Method are of a type called *qualitative*. For general details on qualitative interviewing, the reader is invited to consult the vast extant literature on the topic. Nevertheless, there are some specific recommendations on how to conduct the interviews as required by the FSM Method, which we would like to present below.

Length and format. A one-hour time slot is recommended for each interview. A one-on-one format is strongly recommended for the interviews: the respondent and the interviewer should be the only two people participating in, and with access to, the interview. In our experience, interviews with multiple respondents result in less candid – and therefore less useful – answers.

Recording and confidentiality. With the permission of the respondent, the interview should be recorded. There are two reasons for this: first, it facilitates its analysis afterward, and second, it allows the interviewer to focus their attention on the conversation, as opposed to note-taking. The interviewer should manage the recorded interviews and the data obtained from it with the utmost concern and respect for confidentiality for both the individual respondent and the organization. The use of encryption is recommended to protect the audio recording and derived materials. Additionally, no piece of information from an interview should be ever linked to the name of a specific respondent, without their permission.

Structure of the interview. A suggested structure for the interviews is as follows: introduction (~4 min), placement questions (~3 min), open questions (~35 min), semi-open questions (~15 min), wrap-up (~3 min). Obviously, you can play with these structure and adjust it to your personal preference.

During the **introduction**, the interviewer will greet the respondent, introduce himself/herself and explain in general terms the purpose of the interview and the reason for the selection of the respondent, as well as the expected length of the interview. During the introduction, the interviewer will also inform the respondent of his/her rights, request permission to record the interview and clarify any doubts from the respondent may have.

The interviewer then presents a series of **placement questions**: (1) *"What is the name of your current position?"* (2) *"Who do you report directly to?"* and (3) *"Do you participate directly in crafting the overall strategy of your firm?"* The answer to these questions will help the interviewer place the respondent in one of the three levels described above, which will determine some of the questions that will be asked later.

Open Questions

The **open questions** are the most important part of the interview, especially during the early interviews. The questions asked in this part are adapted to the respondent: some research has indicated that those involved in crafting a strategy tend to have a different perception of it than those who were not involved. For this reason, during our interviews, respondents that participate directly in crafting the overall strategy (namely, Level 1 respondent) will be presented with a slightly different set of questions than those who do not (namely, Level 2 and 3 respondents).

When interviewing a **Level 2 or 3** individual, the open question section starts with the following question: *"What would you say are the main activities of your position?"* Some respondents will begin answering this question right away. Others may ask for clarification: *"What do you mean?"* The interviewer can then expand: *"Think of a typical week or month. What are the things that take most of your time and attention?"*

On the other hand, when we interview a Level 1 individual, we will frame the question under different terms: instead of asking the individual to report his/her own activities, we will ask him or her to report on the activities of those individuals under his/her supervision. This recommendation is based on our experience interviewing people involved in crafting the strategy: they tend to mix stated business objectives with their factual execution, and even when asked to discuss specific activities they easily drift into expressing desired results as opposed to actual facts.

Thus, when we are interviewing a **Level 1** individual, we use the following strategy: find out first who reports directly to him/her: *"Could you tell me which positions report directly to you?"* We care more about the positions of these subordinates than their actual names. As the respondent lists these positions, we write them down. Then, for each one of them, we will ask: *"What would you say are the key activities of such-and-such position?"*

Some recommendations for conducting the open questions of any level are given below.

Stay factual. The open questions segment of the interview is the most important. Rich and grounded answers here will provide superior data for later analysis. As one tries to move the discussion from the individuals to the organization, and from actions to underlying strategy, one has to make a conscious effort to keep the conversation anchored on concrete activities (*'what'*). As a way to validate the factuality of each specific activity, one should ask for the means or details of its execution (*'how'*). To understand its purpose whenever it is not evident, one also can ask for clarification on the ideas behind these activities (*'why'*). These "what, how and why" are the main source of information during the data analysis. The interviewer should remember, every time he or she hears about a *'what'*, to ask about its corresponding *'how's*, namely the supporting means or the details of its execution, and to ask about the respective *'why'*, namely the overarching purpose behind the activity.

Find the sweet spot. The objective is to keep the discussion focused on the tacit knowledge on the supply chain strategy, which – in terms of the narrative of the conversation – lie in a *sweet spot* between overarching strategy and day-to-day activities. The interviewer should pay close attention to what the respondent says, and pursue interesting areas that emerge during the conversation, always pondering: *"Is what I'm listening right now helping me understand the tacit ideas that guide and underpin the way they do things?"* Every time the answer is "no", a course correction is needed.

- If the discussion is becoming too strategic, the interviewer should make it more factual by asking about execution. Probe questions that can be used to correct the course here are: *"How do you implement this? How is this actually done? How do you ensure this happens?"*
- If the discussion is getting bogged down into operational detail, it should be moved to a higher level of abstraction. Probes that are useful here include: *"What is the idea behind this? What is the purpose of this? What results have you achieved through this?"*, etc.

Explore further. The interviewer should listen carefully to the answers, taking notes of the activities that are mentioned. For each answer, the interviewer will ask for further details. Every time the respondent mentions something of interest, the interviewer should make a note of it and, at the first opportunity, ask for further details: *"You mentioned before something that caught my attention. (Mention it here). Can you tell me more about this?"* To keep the conversation clear, the interviewer should move to clarify things every time the respondent becomes too vague in his / her answers, by asking: *"What do you mean by this? Can you give me an example?"*

The interviewer should allow the open question conversation to run for as long as it has momentum, even if it consumes the rest of the hour. Particularly in the early interviews, when the facilitator is just learning about the organization's activities, letting the open question discussion run its own course is a practical way to collect good qualitative data on the organization's tacit knowledge of its supply chain strategy.

However, there comes a time when the interviewer wants to present the respondent with some more structured questions, either because the open discussion has lost steam or because it is just treading territory that has already been covered in previous interviews to the point of repetition. In these cases, the interviewer is advised to move to the semi-open questions.

Semi-open questions

As you proceed through the interviews, **semi-open** questions become more important. Semi-open questions can serve two purposes. One is to rekindle a dwindling discussion. The other is to explore a particular area of interest about which the interviewer has heard previously and which deserves further exploration. The interviewer should be careful, however, not to mention the name of any previous respondent.

The interviewer should keep at hand a short list of general purpose semi-structured questions. Each one of them should be considered optional, in the sense that the interviewer should only ask those questions that seem relevant to the respondent and that have not been answered before during the course of the present interview. Semi-structured questions that we have used recently include the following: (1) *"What would you say is the biggest opportunity facing you today?"* (2) *"What would you say* is the biggest challenge facing your function today?" (3) "What would you say is your business?" Sometimes this question requires clarification: "In other words, what is it that you sell? What do you provide the customer? What is your value proposition?" (4) "Who is your customer?" (5) "What are the needs of these customers? And how do you satisfy these needs?"

Wrap-up. Some minutes before the hour is over, or when the interviewer decides that the interview has come to an end, the interviewer will wrap-up the interview, thanking the respondent and leaving the door open for further contact if necessary.

Example

A total of 22 interviews were conducted over a month. Some of them were as short as 25 minutes, and others as long as 70 minutes; most were around an hour long. They were conducted over the phone, recorded digitally with permission, and encrypted immediately after completion.

Step 3 – Identify areas, policies and choices

The next step is to identify policies and choices in different areas. For this, the facilitator will listen to each interview and conduct these tasks:

Task 1: Identify tentative areas

Listening to the interviews, the facilitator will try to identify broad ***Areas*** of interest or activity for the organization's supply chain. Once a tentative area of interest or activity is identified in the words of a respondent, the facilitator should write it down. Once they are confirmed, the collection of these areas of activity and interest, will define the **thematic range** of the supply chain strategy of the organization.

Task 2: Identify policies and choices in each area

Policies and Choices are the 'What?' that is taking place within each area. As the facilitator continues listening to the interviews, he or she will try to identify – in each area of activity or interest – the *ongoing policies* that the organization has in place, and the *discrete choices* that the organization has made in that area.

If the interview was conducted attentively, the interviewer should have probed for specific activities every time the respondent mentioned a new area of activity. From these activities we will be able to learn about the policies and choices of the organization. We recommend writing down in a list these policies and choices in the form of imperative statements, starting with a verb.

Task 3: Confirm validity of policies and choices

For a policy or choice to remain in the list, there has to be enough evidence that it exists in practice. Evidence, for example, could be details about operational practices that are in place to support these policies and choices. Operational practices are the *'How?'* of each policy and choice.

The interviewer should listen to the interviews for answers to questions like: *"How is this policy or choice being implemented? How is it being achieved in the field? What is being done to make it happen?"* An experienced interviewer will have asked these questions at the time of the interview. One should also look for additional details that may indicate a policy or choice is actually taking place.

Whenever support for a given policy or choice cannot be found, its validity should be questioned and it should be removed from the list. Only policies and choices for which supporting operational practices, means and details can be determined should remain in the list. Those supporting operational practices, details and means should also be captured in the list, as a reminder of that validity.

Example

The following example from Libica illustrates this step. A respondent told us that Libica offers solutions to small, independent retailers to *"make their store more efficient ... make them as efficient as a big chain."* As a tentative area, we write down 'Independent Retailers'. Looking for policies and choices that fall under this area, we found in the same interview that Libica *"provides independent retailers with access to an inventory management system"*. Additional details on the capabilities of the inventory solution were provided to us in subsequent interviews, from other respondents.

Having found evidence supporting this policy/choice, we retained it.

This is repeated in multiple interviews. Other policies and choices regarding *Independent Retailers* were identified and added to the list. The summary of these policies and choices, along with their supporting operational practices, means or details, is shown in the itemized list below:

- *Give independent retailers access to state-of-the-art inventory management*
    - *Our software replenishes using a grouping logic*
    - *Based on sales, our software adjusts the replenishment levels every day*
    - *Our software takes seasonality in consideration for replenishment*
- *Help independent retailers sell the most profitable products*
    - *Help independent retailers to find missed opportunities in their previous orders and to learn from them*
    - *Help independents place orders for the most profitable commodity products*
- *Help independent retailers get reimbursed*
    - *Help them sell the right products to maximize reimbursements*
    - *Speed up the payment, as they get a direct deposit instead of check*
    - *Double check that they are getting reimbursed the right amount*
- *Help independent retailers create alternate revenue streams*
    - *Launch programs to help independents develop businesses beyond baseline products*
    - *Help independents get reimbursed for providing products to subsidized customers*
- *Let independent retailers tap into the advantages of our size and capabilities*
    - *Negotiate and contract reimbursement rates on their behalf*
    - *Offer private label products under the Libica Label for independent stores*
    - *Offer independent retailers the help of advisers familiar with their regions to coach them on being more profitable*
- *Help independent retailers improve their market share*
    - *Help them market and advertise their stores to local communities*
- *Help independent retailers focus on serving their customers*
    - *Hire a team of business consultants to help independents use our services*

- o   *Offer front-store services to independent retailers, to maximize sales of non-specialty products, etc.*
- o   *Take care of resolving any claim of wrong or late reimbursement*
- *Offer independent retailers capital management services*
  - o   *Offer them aggregate pricing*
  - o   *Finance their operations*
- *Help independent stores transition between owners*
  - o   *Help find a buyer for the store when current owner wants to retire*

Step 4 – Identify objectives & build hierarchy

The next step is to identify the objectives behind the policies and choices, and then to prepare a hierarchical summary for each area.

Task 1: Look for the objectives

Objectives are the *'Why?'* behind the policies and choices. Each policy and choice that has been written down should, in theory, serve a purpose. To find this purpose, the interviewer should examine – based on the interview recording or transcript – what objective, if any, is the organization pursuing through each policy or choice.

For this, the interviewer should listen to the interviews for answers to questions like: *"Why is this policy in place? What is the reason behind this choice? What objective is being pursued?"* An experienced interviewer will have asked these questions at the time of the interview. It may be possible to identify general objectives (what we call **Principles**), as well as more immediate specific objectives (what we call **Imperatives**).

Task 2: Prepare a hierarchical summary per area

A summary should be prepared for the concepts identified in each area of interest or activity. We recommend building each summary using a hierarchical structure, with general objectives (*Principles*) on top, then followed by specific objectives (*Imperatives*), and finally by the Policies and Choices within each area.

Example

The following example from Libica illustrates the output of this step for the 'Independent Retailers' area. Notice the three levels of concepts.

- **Help independent retailers be more competitive**
  - Help independent retailers be more profitable
    - *Help independent retailers sell the most profitable products*
    - *Help independent retailers get reimbursed*
    - *Help independent retailers create alternate revenue streams*
  - Help independent retailers enjoy some of the benefits of larger companies
    - *Let independent retailers tap into the advantages of our size and capabilities*
    - *Give independent retailers access to state-of-the-art inventory management*
    - *Help independent retailers improve their market share*
  - Make it easier for independent retailers to conduct their businesses
    - *Help independent retailers focus on serving their customers*
    - *Offer independent retailers capital management services*
    - *Help independent stores transition between owners*

Step 5 – Build partial maps

Partial maps are a graphical representation of the hierarchical summaries prepared in the previous step. For each area, the hierarchical summary is translated into a conceptual map, e.g. a diagram composed of text located inside boxes, which are then connected through lines showing the relationship between them. Given the hierarchical structure of the summary prepared in the previous step, its translation into a partial map is a very straightforward process.

Example

Consider for example the partial map shown in Figure 19, which corresponds to the area discussed: *'Independent Retailers.'* Compare the structure of the map and the hierarchical summary above.

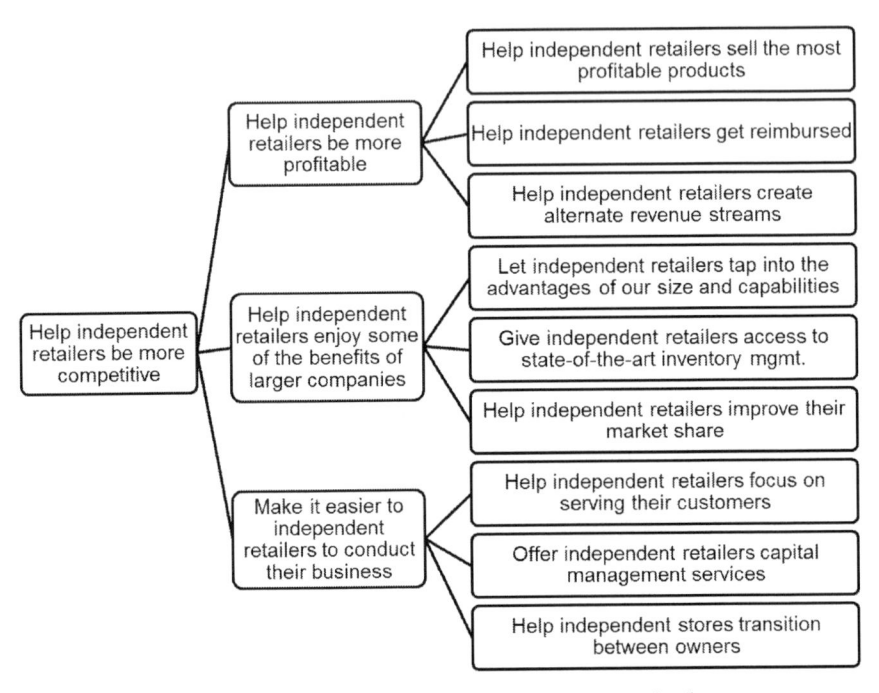

Figure 19: Partial map for area "Independent Retailers"

Step 6 - Validate partial maps

The objective of this step is to confirm that the information used to build the partial maps, which was collected in the interviews about areas, objectives, policies and choices, is an accurate representation of the organization's supply chain strategy. This validation involves presenting all the partial maps, one at a time to a team from the organization's supply chain, including representatives from the supply-chain relevant areas. The team is asked to provide feedback, first individually and then as a group, on whether what is articulated by the maps correspond to what the organization does. Based on the group's input, the partial maps are revised to improve their validity. The scheduled time for the meeting should allow for enough time for discussion. In our experience, a session of 4 hours should suffice.

Example

The partial maps were validated through individual feedback and panel discussion. As individuals first, and then as a panel, 20 members of Libica were asked to consider whether the partial map was a fair summary of the activities the firm performs. Extensive notes were taken on the group's feedback. Changes were made to the partial maps as needed.

Step 7 - Combine related partial maps

The group of partial maps is examined to find whether some of the maps cover strongly related areas. Every time two or more partial maps deal with strongly related areas, an attempt should be made to combine them into a single partial map. The objective of this merging of partial maps is to reduce the complexity of the final output: the functional strategy map is easier to use if closely related areas are grouped under common headings.

The amount of efforts invested in combining areas of activity depends, to some extent, on the total number of areas. As a rule of thumb, we suggest having no more than a dozen areas of activity.

Example

In the case of Libica, partial maps of strongly related areas were combined. For example, among the areas of activity we had identified were two about delivery: one of them included activities about how to *'Deliver exactly what was ordered, within committed volumes'*, and the other one included activities about how to *'Deliver daily, fast, reliably and predictably'*. We combined the contents of these two areas into a single new area, given their shared focus on delivery logistics. To these we also added some activities dealing with *'Increase the speed of our delivery to the market'* that had been misplaced in another area. The overall objective (or *Principle*) of the resulting area was written as *'Deliver fast, accurately and reliably,'* since this statement seemed to reflect the idea behind all the activities and means that were now encompassed under this new area.

Step 8 – Map nominal strategy

The analysis now moves to the nominal strategy of the organization. This step, aims to identify both the **Core** strategy statement of the organization and its supporting strategic **Pillars**, and then map them conceptually. Through the sponsor of the project, the facilitator should negotiate access to written documents stating the organization's core strategy and its espoused strategic pillars. *"Documents and declarations about the firm that are meant for broad distribution"*, even internally, *"can provide useful insights into the image of the firm that the authors seek to project"* (Harrison, 2004, p.93) to their audience – in this case the employees of the organization. In these documents, the core strategy and the strategic pillars are usually easy to identify: they tend to feature prominently in the organization's stated strategy.

Example

We then created an abstract of Libica's business strategy. When asked about their stated strategy, our sponsor - Libica's EVP of Operations and Supply Chain – gave us access to strategic documents where we identified the core strategy and the strategic themes of Libica. After validating these elements with our sponsor, we prepared the conceptual map shown in Figure 20.

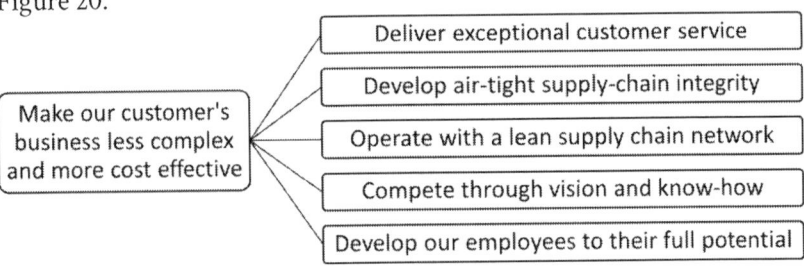

Make our customer's business less complex and more cost effective
- Deliver exceptional customer service
- Develop air-tight supply-chain integrity
- Operate with a lean supply chain network
- Compete through vision and know-how
- Develop our employees to their full potential

Figure 20: Mapped nominal strategy of Libica

Step 9 - Assemble the FSM

Assembling a Functional Strategy Map out of the elements prepared thus far is rather straightforward. One can place the nominal map prepared in Step 8 above the collection of the partial maps prepared in Steps 2 through 7. The resulting Functional Strategy Map features two distinct halves. One half of the map shows a conceptualization of the nominal strategy of the organization. The other half of the map shows a conceptualization of the executed strategy.

Example

We assembled Libica's FSM out of the elements prepared thus far. Because the map is rotated, we placed on the left hand the nominal map prepared in Step 8, and on the right hand the first two layers of all the partial maps prepared in Steps 2 through 7.

Step 10 - Validate FSM

The validation of the Functional Strategy Map takes place in two steps: individual feedback, and collective feedback. In our experience, these can be conducted effectively through discussion with members of the team either remotely by means of the Internet, for example or in a physical meeting.

First round: Individual feedback

In the first round, the Functional Strategy Map assembled in Step 9 can be individually presented to each member of the target firm that was interviewed, along with the question: *'In your opinion, is this abstraction an accurate representation of what the organization does, in general terms?'* Individuals are asked to send their feedback directly to the facilitator.

By now, the facilitator will have sufficient knowledge of the organization's activities, both from the interviews and the validation session, to judge the merits of the feedback.

The facilitator should retain, on a tentative basis, feedback that seems to be based on fact, for further discussion with the group. The facilitator should, nevertheless, disregard pressure to embellish the map by removing unflattering features that are grounded in fact.

Second round: Collective feedback

The individual feedback is discussed with the group in a physical meeting. In our experience, a two-hour time slot will suffice. All members of the group are provided a copy of the revised strategy map, showing whatever tentative modifications were made on the map based on the individual feedback.

It is the facilitator's task to balance two factors: keeping the map faithful to the activities on the ground, and allowing the team to express the ideas in terms that are familiar to them. It is important, after all, that the team members identify the map as an accurate representation of the objectives, policies and choices of the supply chain strategy of the organization.

After this collective feedback session has concluded, and all the recommended changes have been done to the FSM, the final version is distributed to the members of the team.

Example

Libica's FSM was validated through panel discussion. Individuals were asked whether, in their opinion, the FSM was an accurate representation of the objectives, policies and choices of the business unit's supply chain. The feedback of individuals, while kept anonymous, was then discussed in a panel discussion. The map was revised as needed. The resulting FSM is shown in Figure 17, back in Chapter 4. The boundary between the nominal and executed strategies is denoted by a dotted line.

CHAPTER 6

evaluation criteria

Once we have captured the current supply chain strategy of the organization, it will be in the form of a conceptual map such as that shown in Figure 17 (page 42). The conceptual map is like the X-ray plate of a patient for a doctor, or an as-built blueprint for an engineer: it is a factual description of the current state, a snapshot of how things are right now. But it is not an assessment or evaluation of this current state: the doctor still has to diagnose the patient's ailment; the engineer still has to evaluate the as-is design. That is the next step. The same for us: after capturing the current supply chain strategy of an organization, we must move to the task of evaluating it. But, how can this evaluation be done?

Rumelt's Challenge

Back in 1979, Richard Rumelt – a scholar of business strategy – asked a very fundamental question about strategy evaluation, in the form of an "idealized problem." We call it Rumelt's Challenge. Reworded in terms of supply chain strategy, it goes as follows:

> *Suppose one is given reasonably comprehensive descriptions of an organization, its overall strategy, its supply chain and its environment; suppose one is also given a supply chain strategy for consideration. What are the legitimate grounds for evaluating*

> *this supply chain strategy and to what theories, knowledge or models can one turn for help in making such an evaluation?*

Rumelt's Challenge, thus reworded in terms of supply chain strategy, presents us with basic questions for which the current supply chain management literature has no established answers. It is a straightforward yet challenging question: how can we evaluate the merits and weaknesses of a given supply chain strategy? And what criteria can we use for doing this evaluation?

Our Approach

As part of the Supply Chain 2020 Project, we developed an approach for the evaluation of the supply chain strategy. In line with our philosophy, outlined in Chapter 1, our approach to evaluation makes no use of 'best practices' and relies heavily on the internal wisdom of the organization. To use a phrase coined by Rumelt, our approach is based on "evaluation criteria that are context free – that are always valid."

Based on our experience, and on a close review of the literature about the evaluation of business strategy (particularly Tilles 1963, Rumelt 1979, Andrews 1991 and Porter 1996), we propose a set of basic evaluation criteria that are always valid, and that can be useful to identify the strengths and weaknesses of any supply chain strategy, independent of its industry.

This chapter is dedicated to presenting these evaluation criteria. The next chapter will illustrate their use in the evaluation of the supply chain strategy of an organization.

Evaluation Criteria

We propose the following set of criteria for the evaluation of the supply chain strategy of an organization.

Coverage

The first criterion that we would like to propose is what we call *coverage*. The idea of coverage is simple: a good supply chain strategy must be comprehensive. That is to say, it must address –or *cover* – each and every area of decision that matters for the supply chain of the organization. A supply chain strategy with poor coverage, i.e. one that is not comprehensive, because it fails to address – or cover – one or more important areas of decision, cannot be deemed good, because of these blind spots in key areas.

Since coverage is about avoiding blind spots in the supply chain strategy, its evaluation relies on expert knowledge of what areas matter to the supply chain of a given organization. Coverage is about examining whether the topics that are critical for a strategy have been identified and are being addressed.

Clarity

The second criterion that we propose is what we call *clarity*. The idea is pretty straightforward, too: the supply chain strategy of an organization must be clear. For this, the strategy must not only be made *explicit*, but it should also be made *clear*. Since we define a supply chain strategy as a collection of objectives, policies and choices, it follows that a supply chain strategy cannot be clear unless each one of the objectives, policies and choices that compose it are clear. Each objective, policy and choice in the SC strategy must be clearly understood by those making decisions based on them.

Feasibility

The supply chain strategy of an organization must also be *feasible*. This means that each one of its objectives, policies and choices must, in turn, be feasible. In this context, being feasible means being realizable in practice given the competencies and resources (physical, human, financial, technological, etc.) available to the organization, and the constraints of its setting. Described as "appropriateness in the light of available resources" by Tilles, feasibility is our third evaluation criterion.

Internal Consistency

Besides being comprehensive, clear and feasible, the supply chain strategy of an organization must be consistent with itself. This property – which we call *internal consistency* – is one of the most fundamental of all strategy evaluation criteria. It refers to things like "fit, unity, coherence, compatibility and synergy" (Andrews, 1991) among the different objectives, policies and choices that compose a supply chain strategy. We have found it useful to think about the internal consistency of a supply chain strategy in terms of three levels: compatibility, coherence and synergy.

Compatibility

The most basic level of internal consistency, what we call *compatibility*, is about avoiding what Rumelt (1979) calls "gross inconsistencies" within a strategy. At a minimum, the different objectives, policies and choices in a supply chain strategy are expected to be compatible with each other. If these objectives, policies or choices are not able to co-exist, then we have a compatibility problem, which is the most severe form of internal inconsistency. Compatibility is our fourth evaluation criterion.

Coherence

Being able to coexist, however, is not sufficient: it is important that different elements of the supply chain strategy don't cancel each other out. The next level of internal consistency, what we call *coherence*, refers to reduced antagonism among the different objectives, policies or choices in the supply chain strategy. The idea of coherence is that these different objectives, policies and choices in a strategy "cumulate or do not erode" (Porter, 1996) – or at least erode as little as possible – each other's positive cumulative impact on the overall goals. Coherence is our fifth criterion.

"A key function of strategy is to provide coherence to organizational action", says Rumelt (1979), and warns that "problems of strategic inconsistency" may result in "conflict" and "bickering" across functions. Our experience shows that this is true also in supply chain strategy. One way to promote coherence among seemingly competing objectives or policies is to establish a clear *precedence*, or pecking order, among them.

Synergy

It is good that the objectives, policies and choices that make up a supply chain strategy are not downright incompatible or mutually detrimental.

But it is even better if they can work harmoniously, reinforcing each other's strengths. This is the third level of internal consistency, which we call *synergy*. Synergy is the presence of desirable reinforcing relationships – preferably mutual, but not necessarily so – between the objectives, policies or choices in the supply chain strategy. This way, they by mutually reinforcing each other, the positive impact they have on supporting the overall strategy of the organization is amplified. This is our sixth evaluation criterion of the goodness of a supply chain strategy.

Coherence and synergy are – to a large extent – like two sides of the same coin. However, there is an important difference between them: whereas an absence of synergy is acceptable, an absence of coherence is not. Think of lack of coherence as 'anti-synergy'. In our experience, most unresolved trade-offs are characterized by the presence of these 'anti-synergy' among concepts (i.e. among objectives, policies or choices.)

External Consistency

Besides being consistent with itself, a good supply chain strategy of an organization must also be consistent with the outside, with the context in which it operates. This expectation that a strategy should "both match and be adapted to its environment" is called "consonance" by Rumelt (1979). We call it *external consistency*, and we present it as the seventh criterion to evaluate the merits of a supply chain strategy. The environment with which the supply chain strategy should be consistent includes not only the rest of the organization, but also the market and industry in which it competes, or – in the case of non-competitive organizations – the setting in which it operates. It also includes the world at large. "Consistency with the environment" – described by Tilles (1963) as an "important test of strategy" – is about whether its components "really make sense with respect to what is going on outside", both "now" and "in the future".

Support

A supply chain strategy may be both clear and feasible, it may be comprehensive, it may be consistent with itself and its environment, and still not be any good if it provides no *support* to the overall strategy of the organization. The whole *reason of being* for the supply chain strategy of an organization is to support its overall strategy. For this to happen, each component of the supply chain strategy – each objective, each policy and each choice – must, in some way, either directly or indirectly, provide support (that is to say enable, advance or help realize) some element of the overall strategy. This is our eighth evaluation criterion. Any component of the supply chain strategy that provides no support – directly or indirectly – to the overall strategy, or whose net support is negative, should be either eliminated from the supply chain strategy, or modified so that this is corrected.

Sufficiency

It is not enough for each one of the components of a supply chain strategy to provide some support to the overall strategy. It is necessary for them, as a group, to support it *sufficiently*. Our ninth evaluation criterion, which we call *sufficiency*, refers to the expectation that each one of the overall objectives that have been set for the supply chain of the organization be fully satisfied, and that the overall strategy of the organization be sufficiently supported by the supply chain. Sufficiency should be realizable by the combined support provided to the overall strategy by all the objectives, policies and choices in the supply chain strategy.

Parsimony

As we have stated above, a supply chain strategy should provide the expected support to the overall strategy, given the constraints and possibilities of the environment. However, if there is more than one way to achieve the same level of support, given the same constraints and with all other things being equal, preference should be given to the one that requires the less resources (time, money, effort, etc.) *Parsimony*, the notion that the supply chain strategy should only use the resources that are necessary to provide the expected level of support to the overall strategy, is our tenth evaluation criterion.

Riskiness

Because of environmental uncertainty, market dynamics and incomplete information, among other factors, every supply chain strategy has a certain level of risk. A good supply chain strategy should not represent more risk to the organization than it is willing to face. This is what Tilles (1963) called an "acceptable degree of risk" and Andrews (1991) later described as a "feasible ... level of risk". We refer to this notion as riskiness, and it is our twelfth evaluation criterion: a good supply chain strategy should not represent more risk than the organization is willing to accept.

Advantageousness

Some supply chains (but not all) serve overall strategies that are competitive in nature. In the case of organizations operating in competitive settings, having a supply chain strategy that can help them realize a competitive advantage against others is highly desirable. This is what we call *advantageousness*, a criterion that applies to supply chains in competitive settings, regarding whether the supply chain strategy provides the organization a unique differentiating competitive advantage. A supply chain strategy is advantageous if it has the ability to provide, through the supply chain, an additional competitive advantage to the organization.

Actionability

The last evaluation criterion that we propose applies mostly to supply chain strategies that are not in place yet, but are being considered for implementation. We call it *actionability*. It refers to the idea that, in order to help bridge the gap between overall strategy and supply chain operations, the supply chain strategy should be actionable enough. In other words, at its lower levels of abstraction, near the operations end of the spectrum, the supply chain strategy should be specific enough to serve as a good guide for taking actions. A good supply chain strategy is actionable.

In the next chapter we will see how these criteria can be used to evaluate the supply chain strategy of an organization.

CHAPTER 7

applying the criteria

The evaluation criteria are useful to the extent they can be actually applied in the evaluation of a supply chain strategy. In this section we present how we have applied the evaluation criteria presented above to the evaluation of supply chain strategies in past projects.

For an existing supply chain strategy, the evaluation process is conducted after the *capture* process has been completed. The evaluation uses as its starting point the validated FSM that describes this current supply chain strategy. Alternatively, a supply chain strategy that is not currently in place but is being considered for future implementation, can also be evaluated, as long as it is expressed in the form of a FSM.

To conduct the evaluation, we must assemble a team of experts that are familiar with the supply chain of the organization. These experts should also be familiar with the FSM of the supply chain strategy that will be evaluated. Preferably, they will have been involved in the capture process. The evaluation is done by these experts working first individually, and then as a team, and is facilitated by a neutral, independent facilitator.

Coverage

As we mentioned back in page 64, the criterion of *coverage* postulates that a good supply chain strategy must be comprehensive, without blind spots, addressing all the areas of decision that matters for the supply chain of the organization. *Coverage* is assessed by asking the individual experts, separately, what areas of interest are not currently being addressed by the supply chain strategy, as described in the FSM. The answers of the individual experts are collected and shared with the group, without attribution to the individuals that provided them. These answers are then discussed and expanded in a panel discussion with the whole group of experts.

The explicit nature of the FSM makes it relatively easy to identify the areas of interest that *are* being addressed by the supply chain strategy, thus making it also relatively easy for a group of experts familiar with the supply chain of the organization to identify the areas of interest that *are not* being addressed (e.g. that are absent from the FSM).

In our projects so far there has not been a need for a mechanism more refined than this to evaluate *coverage*. A provision we have found useful is taking extensive notes, while the FSM is being built, of all comments regarding: (a) things the business unit could be doing but is not, and (b) areas that seem relevant, for which the business unit has no clear established policy. These comments may indicate shortcomings in coverage.

Examples

As a ***first example***, let us mention the first supply chain strategy evaluation exercise we conducted. It was done with Unit-X, a business unit of a specialty chemical manufacturer, the subject of our first project on the subject of rethinking a supply chain strategy.

Evaluation of their supply chain strategy was the second in a three-part project: the other two parts were capture and reformulation. Although the whole project lasted two years, the evaluation phase lasted only two months. As part of the evaluation phase, a group of experts from the supply chain function were asked to consider, first individually and then as a panel, the FSM that was prepared for Unit-X. Its second, third and fourth levels are shown in Figure 21. They were convened as a panel for half a day to evaluate the supply chain strategy, based on the FSM.

72 | MIT SCS LAB

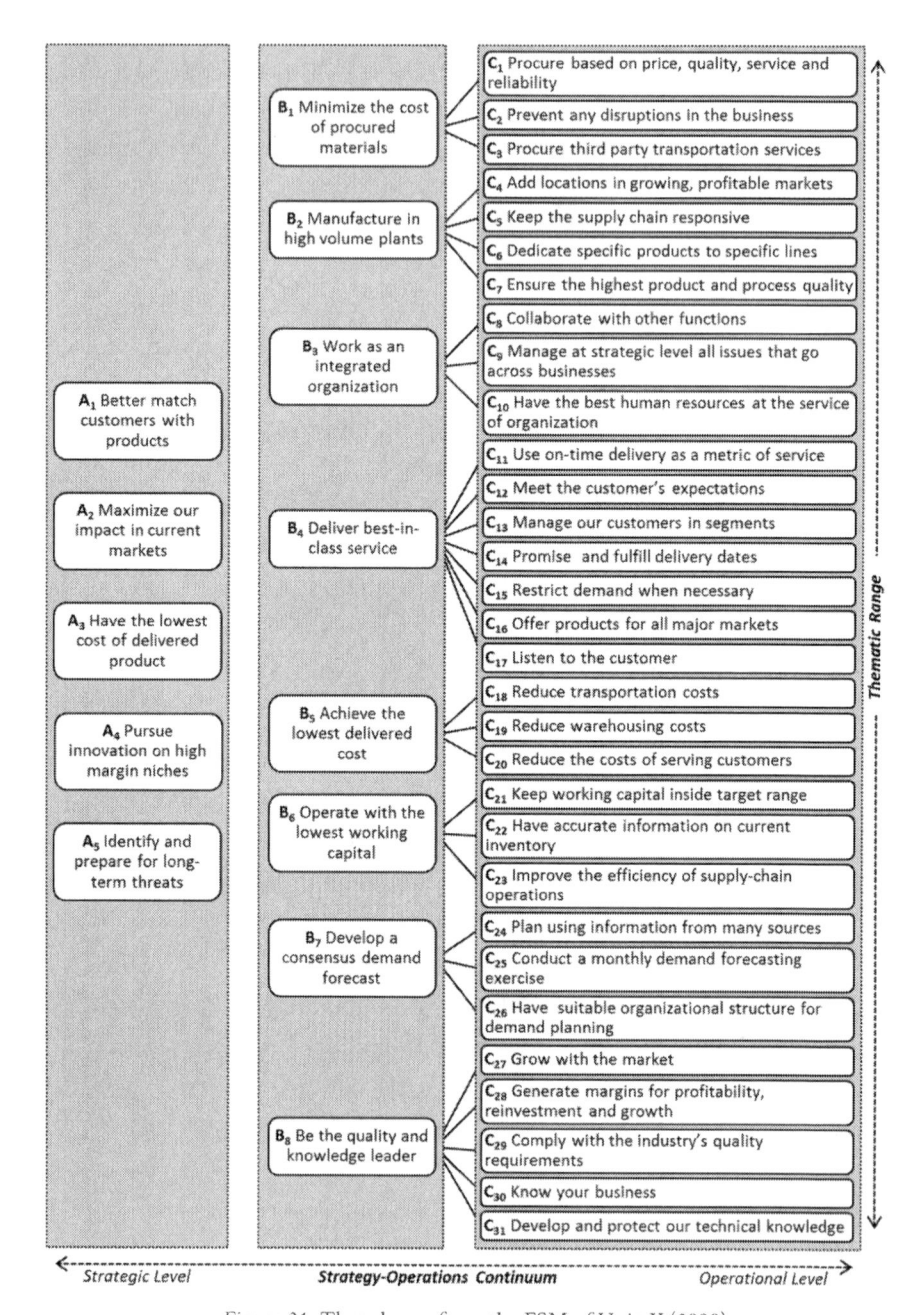

Strategic Level

- A₁ Better match customers with products
- A₂ Maximize our impact in current markets
- A₃ Have the lowest cost of delivered product
- A₄ Pursue innovation on high margin niches
- A₅ Identify and prepare for long-term threats

Strategy-Operations Continuum

- B₁ Minimize the cost of procured materials
  - C₁ Procure based on price, quality, service and reliability
  - C₂ Prevent any disruptions in the business
  - C₃ Procure third party transportation services
- B₂ Manufacture in high volume plants
  - C₄ Add locations in growing, profitable markets
  - C₅ Keep the supply chain responsive
  - C₆ Dedicate specific products to specific lines
  - C₇ Ensure the highest product and process quality
- B₃ Work as an integrated organization
  - C₈ Collaborate with other functions
  - C₉ Manage at strategic level all issues that go across businesses
  - C₁₀ Have the best human resources at the service of organization
- B₄ Deliver best-in-class service
  - C₁₁ Use on-time delivery as a metric of service
  - C₁₂ Meet the customer's expectations
  - C₁₃ Manage our customers in segments
  - C₁₄ Promise and fulfill delivery dates
  - C₁₅ Restrict demand when necessary
  - C₁₆ Offer products for all major markets
  - C₁₇ Listen to the customer
- B₅ Achieve the lowest delivered cost
  - C₁₈ Reduce transportation costs
  - C₁₉ Reduce warehousing costs
  - C₂₀ Reduce the costs of serving customers
- B₆ Operate with the lowest working capital
  - C₂₁ Keep working capital inside target range
  - C₂₂ Have accurate information on current inventory
  - C₂₃ Improve the efficiency of supply-chain operations
- B₇ Develop a consensus demand forecast
  - C₂₄ Plan using information from many sources
  - C₂₅ Conduct a monthly demand forecasting exercise
  - C₂₆ Have suitable organizational structure for demand planning
- B₈ Be the quality and knowledge leader
  - C₂₇ Grow with the market
  - C₂₈ Generate margins for profitability, reinvestment and growth
  - C₂₉ Comply with the industry's quality requirements
  - C₃₀ Know your business
  - C₃₁ Develop and protect our technical knowledge

Operational Level

Thematic Range

Figure 21: Three layers from the FSM of Unit-X (2008)

Participants remarked that, through examination of the FSM, their supply chain strategy was not properly addressing several areas of interest for Unit-X, namely innovation, collaboration and organizational structure. These gaps were described by them as 'shortcomings in coverage,' which suggested to us the idea of *coverage* as an evaluation criterion in the first place.

A ***second example*** comes from our project with Libica, which we have already mentioned before. It was the second project we conducted on the subject of rethinking a supply chain strategy. Several of Libica's supply chain experts examined the FSM shown in Figure 17. Since they we had helped prepare it, being involved in the *capture* process, they knew the FSM was a thorough summary of their current supply chain strategy. Through examination of this FSM, some experts realized that their strategy had nothing to say about collaborating with customers, an area that they considered increasingly important for their supply chain.

Clarity

As we mentioned back in page 65, the criterion of *clarity* postulates that a good supply chain strategy must be explicit and clear; this in turn requires each one of its objectives, policies and choices to be clear to those making decisions based on them. *Clarity* is assessed by asking the experts, individually, whether any of the objectives, policies and choices that make up the supply chain strategy, as described in the FSM, is not clear. As we did for coverage, the answers of the individual experts are collected and shared with the group, without attribution to the individuals that provided them. These collected and anonymized answers are then discussed and expanded in the panel discussion with the whole group of experts. So far, we have not required a mechanism more refined than this.

Examples

In both our Libica and Unit-X projects, the group of experts assessing the clarity of the concepts in their respective FSM were also involved in the capture process. Possibly because of this, there were no clarity issues when evaluating their current supply chain strategies based on the FSMs.

Later in our project with Unit-X, something happened that made us realize both the importance and relativity of *clarity*. The president of Unit-X had hired a consulting firm to help develop a new vision for the business unit. The resulting vision statement, shared with us, laid out "four key business goals" for Unit-X, written in a way that their first letters spelled out GROW. To achieve this acrostic, the first goal started with the phrase *"Grow spread"* and the third one with the phrase *"Own quality"*. Although unintelligible to others, including us as external facilitators, the meaning of these two phrases was very clear to the supply chain experts of Unit-X: "Grow spread" meant to increase the difference between the cost of producing a good and the price it commands from the customer, and "Own quality" meant to take personal responsibility for ensuring the high quality of the product and technical service delivered to the customer. When these two phrases were used as part of their revised supply chain strategy, the team was clear regarding their meaning.

Feasibility

As we mentioned back in page 65, the criterion of *feasibility* postulates that a good supply chain strategy must be feasible, which in turn requires each one of its objectives, policies and choices to be feasible. *Feasibility* is assessed by asking the experts, individually, whether any of the objectives, policies and choices that make up the supply chain strategy, as described in the FSM, is feasible. That is to say, whether it is realizable in practice, given the competencies and resources that the organization has or can acquire, and the constraints of its current environment. As with other criteria, the answers of the individual experts are collected and shared with the group, without attribution, and are discussed by the panel of experts. So far, we have not required a mechanism more refined than this.

Examples

Since FSMs are built to characterize current supply chain strategies, they are a reflection of strategy as practice. The concepts in an FSM capture what is *already* in place. Possibly because of this, feasibility has – so far – not come up as a big issue when evaluating the FSMs of *current* supply chain strategies in projects. It may be more relevant as a criterion when evaluating proposed or tentative supply chain strategies that are being considered. For example, in our project with Libica, when the team was considering a new supply chain strategy as a revision to their current one, they decided to "move away from price, and into value and solutions". Before committing to this change in their supply chain strategy, the team discussed whether this objective was feasible. They did so by discussing by what means it could be achieved. Only after its feasibility was established, was the objective accepted as part of the supply chain strategy.

An interesting example of a feasibility issue, not from one of our projects but from a company we are familiar with, is as follows. A food company in Latin America manufactures a portfolio of dairy products, including yogurts in two dozen different flavors. The company distributes and sells its products throughout one of the largest countries in South America. A key channel for them is that of nano-stores: thousands of tiny convenience retailers, with spaces no larger than a typical restroom, located at a rate of four or five per block in the densely populated urban areas of the capital city. According to one of the supply chain executives of this company, a central objective of their supply chain strategy is to have zero stock-outs of any of their products anywhere. I asked the executive to clarify the meaning of this objective, and she confirmed that it meant what I feared it did: for the yogurts alone, for example, it meant ensuring a perfect, 100% stock availability at all times for *each one* of their two dozen yogurt flavors across the thousands of stores – including nano-stores – in the capital city. Perfect availability of product across such a fragmented retailer base would require keeping inventory levels or having replenishment frequencies that are, in reality, not feasible given the financial constraints of the company and the retailers. "Zero stock-outs anywhere" may be useful as a *dogmatic* objective, as an ideal, but it fails as a *pragmatic* objective. In practice, it does not pass the *feasibility* criterion.

Internal Consistency

Internal consistency is evaluated level by level. Within each level, we ask our individual experts, separately, to evaluate whether each concept within a given level is consistent with each other concept in that level.

We have found it useful to prepare questionnaires that include a question for each pair of concepts within a level, and offer answer choices in the form of a Likert scale. Some scales that we have used are provided below. The questionnaires are administered separately to the experts, and their answers are consolidated to be discussed and validated by the group.

A mechanism we have found is useful for summarizing the answers for discussion with the group is to arrange them in the form of a matrix. Since they include data on evaluation, we usually refer to these as 'evaluation matrices'. Examples of these matrices will be provided below.

Below we discuss how we think it is possible to assess internal consistency by asking questions in terms of compatibility, coherence and synergy.

Compatibility

One way to evaluate internal consistency is to ask questions about **compatibility**. For every pair of concepts X and Y within a given layer of the FSM, we can prepare a question of the form "Is [concept X] compatible with [concept Y]?" A set of answer choices that can be used here is:

1. *Yes, they are totally compatible*
2. *They are somewhat compatible*
3. *They are somewhat incompatible*
4. *No, they are totally incompatible*
5. *I am not sure*

This question would be included in the questionnaire to be administered individually to the experts. The answers of each expert can then be coded and aggregated, to calculate – for example – the percentage of the respondents who described the relationship as '*Compatible*' (options 1 and 2), as '*Incompatible*' (options 3 and 4), and as '*Unsure*' (option 5).

RETHINKING YOUR SUPPLY CHAIN STRATEGY | 77

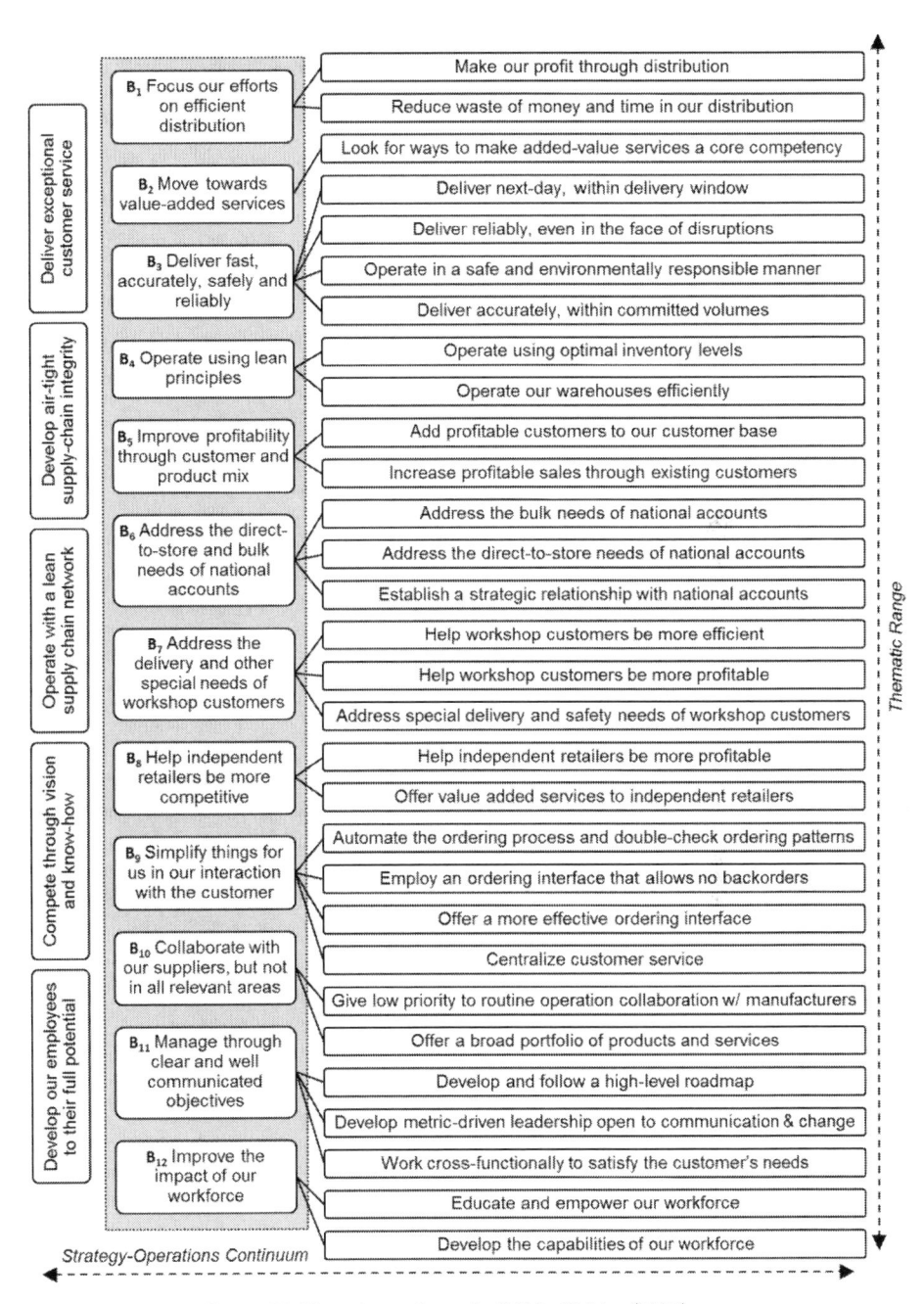

Strategy	Objective	Operation
Deliver exceptional customer service	B₁ Focus our efforts on efficient distribution	Make our profit through distribution
		Reduce waste of money and time in our distribution
	B₂ Move towards value-added services	Look for ways to make added-value services a core competency
		Deliver next-day, within delivery window
	B₃ Deliver fast, accurately, safely and reliably	Deliver reliably, even in the face of disruptions
		Operate in a safe and environmentally responsible manner
		Deliver accurately, within committed volumes
Develop air-tight supply-chain integrity	B₄ Operate using lean principles	Operate using optimal inventory levels
		Operate our warehouses efficiently
	B₅ Improve profitability through customer and product mix	Add profitable customers to our customer base
		Increase profitable sales through existing customers
Operate with a lean supply chain network	B₆ Address the direct-to-store and bulk needs of national accounts	Address the bulk needs of national accounts
		Address the direct-to-store needs of national accounts
		Establish a strategic relationship with national accounts
	B₇ Address the delivery and other special needs of workshop customers	Help workshop customers be more efficient
		Help workshop customers be more profitable
		Address special delivery and safety needs of workshop customers
Compete through vision and know-how	B₈ Help independent retailers be more competitive	Help independent retailers be more profitable
		Offer value added services to independent retailers
	B₉ Simplify things for us in our interaction with the customer	Automate the ordering process and double-check ordering patterns
		Employ an ordering interface that allows no backorders
		Offer a more effective ordering interface
	B₁₀ Collaborate with our suppliers, but not in all relevant areas	Centralize customer service
		Give low priority to routine operation collaboration w/ manufacturers
Develop our employees to their full potential	B₁₁ Manage through clear and well communicated objectives	Offer a broad portfolio of products and services
		Develop and follow a high-level roadmap
		Develop metric-driven leadership open to communication & change
	B₁₂ Improve the impact of our workforce	Work cross-functionally to satisfy the customer's needs
		Educate and empower our workforce
		Develop the capabilities of our workforce

Strategy-Operations Continuum ←——————————————→ *Thematic Range* ↕

Figure 22: Three layers from the FSM of Libica (2009)

Example

Consider the following example, from our project with Libica. Figure 22 shows the second, third and fourth layers of the FSM of Libica (shown originally in Figure 17). In order to facilitate explaining the process of evaluation, we have highlighted the third layer of the map, and labeled its concepts from B_1 through B_{12}. To evaluate the compatibility of the concepts in this layer, we prepared a series of questions, one for each pair of concepts, asking about their mutual compatibility. For example, for the pair of concepts B_1 ("Focus our efforts on efficient distribution") and B_3 ("Deliver fast, accurately, safely and reliably"), there is a corresponding question regarding whether B_1 and B_3 are mutually compatible. In long form, this question can be written as follows: "Is *focusing our efforts on efficient distribution* mutually compatible with *delivering fast, accurately, safely and reliably?*"

A questionnaire containing questions like this for each possible pair of concepts within a given layer was administered individually, in the form of an online survey, to the group of experts. To reduce fatigue, and since our expert team was relatively large (23 members), we gave every expert only half the questions. Their answers were then summarized by calculating what percentage of the respondents had said the two concepts in a given question were *incompatible* (answer options 3 and 4). These percentages are shown in Table 2. In gray are the cells with values higher than 25%, an arbitrary threshold chosen to highlight the greatest values.

Reading this matrix, we learn – for example – that 73% of the respondents expressed the view that B_6 and B_8 are either somewhat or totally incompatible. The matrix itself was shared with the group of experts, but to help them assimilate it, we also expressed the most outstanding incompatibilities in words and graphically. For example, **verbally** we told the group of experts that "Addressing the direct-to-store and bulk needs of national accounts" was judged by them to be at least partly incompatible with "Helping independent retailers be more competitive." We expressed all the incompatibilities greater than 25% in this form, for discussion with them.

RETHINKING YOUR SUPPLY CHAIN STRATEGY | 79

B2	0%										
B3	0%	27%									
B4	0%	0%	0%								
B5	27%	18%	18%	9%							
B6	0%	0%	0%	0%	9%						
B7	9%	0%	9%	0%	15%	38%					
B8	0%	0%	0%	0%	9%	73%	38%				
B9	0%	0%	0%	0%	23%	9%	0%	18%			
B10	0%	0%	0%	0%	10%	18%	0%	0%	18%		
B11	0%	0%	0%	0%	0%	0%	0%	18%	0%	8%	
B12	8%	0%	0%	0%	9%	0%	0%	15%	0%	9%	0%
	B1	B2	B3	B4	B5	B6	B7	B8	B9	B10	B11

Table 2: Summary of compatibility answers for the third level of Libica's FSM

We also represented **graphically** each one of the five greatest incompatibilities found in the matrix, as shown in Figure 23. This graph communicates all five incompatibilities in a clean and concise manner.

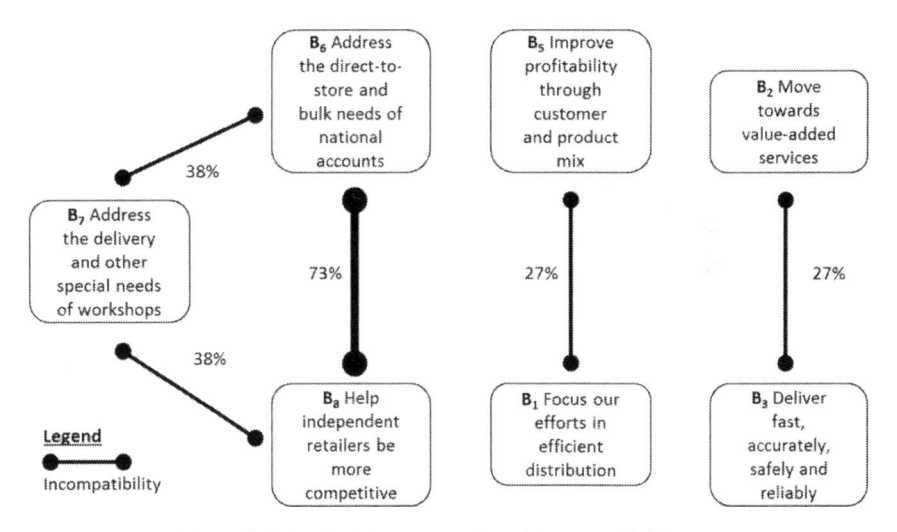

Figure 23: Graphical representation of incompatibilities

The left part of this figure shows a three-way incompatibility among objectives that seek to serve customer segments differently according to their needs while using the same logistics configuration in their supply chain to serve all segments. "To me, it was like a light bulb went off...," said their Senior VP of SC, describing his reaction to the findings of our compatibility evaluation: "We are trying to do everything!"

Coherence and Synergy

Another way to evaluate internal consistency is to ask questions about **coherence** and **synergy**. In past projects, we have found it useful to combine both concepts into a single question. For every pair of concepts X and Y within a given layer of the FSM, we can ask whether concept X "helps" or "reinforces" concept Y. Answer choices could be as follows:

1. *Yes! It provides crucial reinforcement*
2. *Yes. It provides significant reinforcement*
3. *It may provide reinforcement, but only a little*
4. *It makes very little or no difference*
5. *It may be detrimental, but only a little*
6. *No. It is significantly detrimental*
7. *No! It is absolutely detrimental*
8. *I am not sure*

Providing answer options like this allows respondents to indicate, in their response, either the presence of synergy or the absence of coherence. This question would be included in the questionnaire to be administered individually to the experts.

The answers of each expert to the question can then be coded and aggregated. In the past, we have coded the answer options as follows: option 1 is coded as +3 (or even +4), option 2 is coded as +2, option 3 is coded as +1, option 4 is coded as 0, option 5 is coded as -1, option 6 is coded as -2, option 7 is coded as -3 (or even -4), and option 8 is coded as either 0 or left empty.

For each question, the averages of the coded answers from the respondents can then be arranged in the form of a matrix. In this matrix, negative values would indicate a lack of *coherence*, i.e. detrimental interactions between concepts, where one of them is detracting from another.

Likewise, positive values in the matrix would indicate *synergy*. Symmetrical positive values, i.e. positive values that occur in pairs at opposite sides of the long diagonal of the matrix, indicate a mutually reinforcing relationship between concepts.

Examples

Consider the following examples, from our project with Unit-X. Figure 21 shows the second, third and fourth layers of the FSM of Unit-X. In order to facilitate explaining the process of evaluation, we have labeled its concepts: those in the third layer (the middle one in the figure) are labeled from B_1 through B_8. To evaluate the compatibility of the concepts in this layer, we prepared a series of questions exploring whether each of the concepts helps, reinforces or erodes each other concept in the same layer. For example, there is a question that explores whether B_2 ("Manufacture in high volume plants") *helps* B_4 ("Deliver best-in-class service"). In long form, this question can be written as follows: "Does *manufacturing in high volume plants* help us *deliver best-in-class service?*"

As opposed to a question about mutual compatibility, a question about whether a concept reinforces (or erodes) another one is not necessarily bidirectional. So there is a separate question that mirrors this one but has the concepts in the other order, a question that explores whether B_4 *"helps"* B_2, which reads: "Does *delivering best-in-class service* help us *manufacture in high volume plants?*"

A questionnaire containing questions like this for each concept's relationship with every other concept in its layer was administered individually, in the form of an online survey, to the group of experts. Their answers were then coded as stated above, and an average value of the answers was calculated for each of the question. These averages were then arranged in the form of a matrix, which is shown in Table 3.

For each question, besides the average value for the answers, we also calculated the standard deviation of the answers. This would help us identify which answers had the biggest dispersion among respondents, which would suggest areas of disagreement in their assessment of coherence.

	B1	B2	B3	B4	B5	B6	B7	B8
B1		0.6	1.4	-0.1	0.4	-0.4	1.4	0.4
B2	0.5		0.4	-0.5	0.3	-0.2	0.9	1.1
B3	0.0	0.3		0.4	0.4	0.8	1.2	0.4
B4	-0.1	-0.8	2.2		-0.8	-1.2	1.9	1.8
B5	3.0	1.8	1.3	-0.9		0.2	1.7	1.0
B6	2.1	-1.1	1.1	-1.3	0.3		1.6	0.4
B7	0.0	0.0	1.6	0.4	0.0	0.0		0.3
B8	0.1	0.5	1.8	1.0	-0.3	0.0	0.4	

Table 3: Matrix showing average scores for coherence/synergy

In this matrix, each cell refers to a possible relationship where once concept helps/hurts another concept. In the matrix, he column headers indicate the concept exerting the action (the 'active' concept) whereas the row headers refer to the concept receiving the action (the 'passive' concept) in the relationship being evaluated in that cell. Reading this matrix, then, we learn – for example – that, based on the average of the responses from our group of experts, concept B_2 is a little detrimental to concept B_6 (given the average value of -1.1 for this relationship).

To make it easier to derive insights, we decided to identify the cells that had absolute values higher than ½. This is shown in Table 4.

	B1	B2	B3	B4	B5	B6	B7	B8
B1		+	+				+	
B2	+			-			+	+
B3						+	+	
B4		-	+		-	-	+	+
B5	+	+	+	-			+	+
B6	+	-	+	-			+	
B7			+					
B8		+	+	+				

Table 4: Matrix highlighting the stronger positive and negative values

In that matrix, cells with a positive sign indicate that this relationship was assessed as positive (i.e. supportive, helpful, reinforcing) on average, above a +½ threshold. A negative sign, on the other hand, means that this relationship was assessed as negative (i.e. eroding, detrimental) on average, below a -½ threshold.

Both the matrices with numbers and signs were shared with the group of experts. As before, to help them assimilate it, we also expressed the stronger reinforcing and detrimental relationships both in words and graphically. We also shared with the group of experts a summary of reciprocal relationships we identified in the matrix. Table 5 shows the reciprocal positive relationships we found in the matrix, i.e. the cases where a concept both *gives help* and *receives help* above the +½ threshold.

	B1	B2	B3	B4	B5	B6	B7	B8
B1		+	+				+	
B2	+						+	+
B3						+	+	
B4			+				+	+
B5	+	+	+				+	+
B6	+		+				+	
B7			+					
B8			+	+	+			

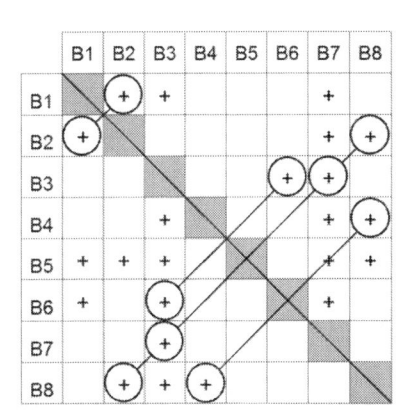

Table 5: Reciprocally reinforcing relationships

Figure 24 represents the same relationships graphically.

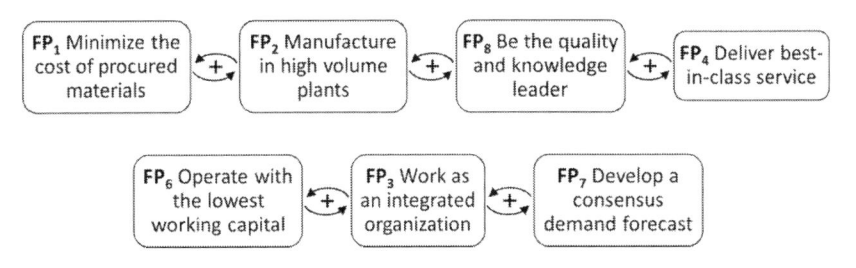

- **FP₁** Minimize the cost of procured materials
- **FP₂** Manufacture in high volume plants
- **FP₈** Be the quality and knowledge leader
- **FP₄** Deliver best-in-class service
- **FP₆** Operate with the lowest working capital
- **FP₃** Work as an integrated organization
- **FP₇** Develop a consensus demand forecast

Figure 24: Reciprocally reinforcing relationships, represented graphically

What Figure 24 reveals is precisely some of the **synergies** that exist within the supply chain strategy of Unit-X. We also looked at the *anti-synergies*, i.e. the instances where a lack of coherence results in mutually detrimental relationships between concepts. Table 6 shows the reciprocal negative relationships we found in the matrix, i.e. the cases where a concept both *hurts* and *is hurt* by another, below the -½ threshold.

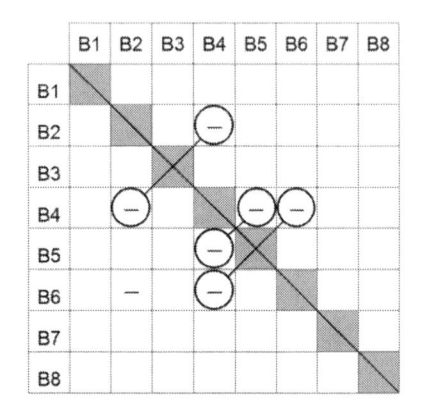

Table 6: Reciprocally detrimental relationships

Figure 25 represents the same detrimental relationships graphically.

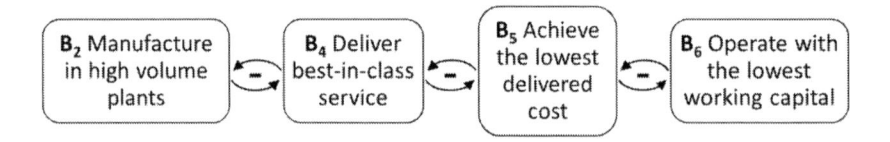

Figure 25: Reciprocally detrimental relationships, represented graphically

What reveals Figure 25 is precisely a lack of **coherence** that exist at the core of Unit-X's supply chain strategy, involving their objectives for manufacturing, inventory levels and customer service. "You've hit the nail on the head," said Unit-X's VP of Supply Chain, adding that "This is a very good crystallization of things." He confirmed that the "conflict is a very, very important item right now", one of "the fundamental issues we're struggling with". In the case of Unit-X, their reticence in establishing a clear **precedence**, a pecking order among these competing objectives, helped perpetuate these conflicts and adversely affected the coherence of their supply chain strategy.

The evaluation of coverage and internal consistency (compatibility, coherence and synergy) takes place within layers of the FSM. For example, consider the three middle layers of Unit-X's FSM as shown in Figure 21. For example, we can evaluate the coverage or internal consistency of the concepts found in the middle layer of the FSM, whose concepts we have labeled B_1 through B_8. We can also evaluate coverage and internal consistency for concepts found in the higher layer, for concepts $A_1 - A_5$, or for the lower layer, for concepts $C_1 - C_{31}$. *Coverage* and *internal consistency* are evaluated along the *thematic range* (Figure 26), a layer at a time.

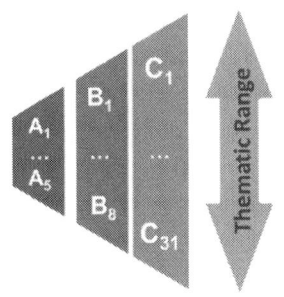

Figure 26: Schematic of Thematic Range for Libica's FSM

Support

Support is evaluated following a logic similar to the one used above, but along the strategy operations continuum, across levels of abstraction (Figure 27). For every pair of concepts on adjacent layers of the FSM, we can prepare a question of the form "Does [the concept in the lower level] *help us* [concept in the higher level]?" Instead of 'help us', we can also ask "Does [lower concept] *help us achieve our goal of* [higher concept]?" For example, in the case of Unit-X's FSM (Figure 21), for each concept between B_1 and B_8, there will be a question asking whether that concept supports each one of the concepts in the layer above them, from A_1 to A_5.

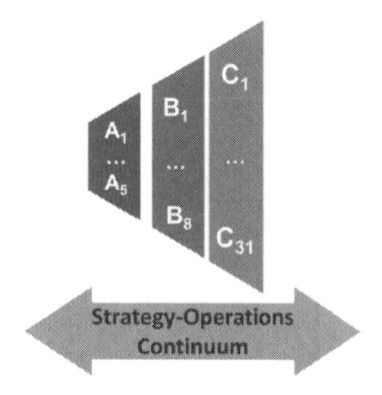

Figure 27: Schematic of Strat-Ops Continuum for Libica's FSM

Likewise, for each concept between C_1 and C_{31}, there will be a question asking whether that concept supports each one of the concepts in the layer above them, from B_1 to B_8 (see Figure 28).

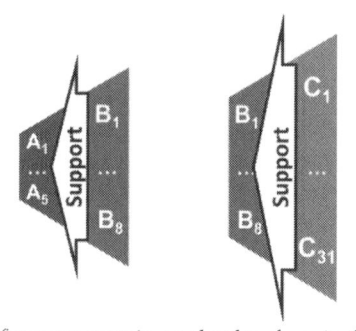

Figure 28: Support from concepts in one level to those in the next higher level

Answer choices for these questions could be as follows:

1. *Yes! It provides crucial support to the goal*
2. *Yes. It provides significant support to the goal*
3. *It provides only a little support to the goal*
4. *It makes no difference for this goal*
5. *It detracts only a little from the goal*
6. *No. It significantly detracts from the goal*
7. *No! It completely detracts from the goal*
8. *I am not sure*

The answers provided by individual respondents to these questions are coded in order to be analyzed. An approach to coding that has proven useful is to calculate the percentage of the respondents who described the relationship as *'Supportive'* (options 1 and 2), as *'Detrimental '* (options 6 and 7), as *'Mostly neutral'* (options 3 through 5) and as *'Unsure'* (option 8).

These four percentages are arranged in four separate matrices. Each value is put in the cell that corresponds to the question for which it was calculated. To facilitate reading the matrices, one may highlight cells that contain values above a certain threshold. No threshold value applies to all instances, so we recommend trying out different thresholds values. In previous projects we have used 50%, 33% and 25% as thresholds, to highlight values that indicate when at least half, a third or a quarter of respondents, respectively, answered in a given way. There are several ways to derive insights from the matrices thus prepared. Sometimes simple inspection will reveal an interesting pattern, whereas in other instances it is useful to express, both verbally and graphically, the relationships that correspond to the highlighted values in each matrix. Verbally, each relationship can be expressed using a statement of the form: *"X% of respondents expressed that Y supports Z;" "X% of respondents expressed Y is detrimental for Z;"* etc. Graphically, several relationships can be expressed using a conceptual diagram, where concepts are depicted as boxes, with lines connecting them to illustrate supportive or detrimental relationships.

Example

Below is an example of evaluating support from our project with Unit-X. In their FSM (Figure 21), the fourth strategic pillar (labeled A_4) reads: *"Pursue innovation on high margin niches."* The third principle (labeled B_3) reads: *"Work as an integrated organization."* The questionnaire, administered to Unit-X's experts individually, included a question about the support B_3 provides to A_4. The question read as follows: "Does *working as an integrated organization* help us to *pursue innovation on high margin niches?"* The experts' answers to this and every other question about evaluation were coded as described above, and matrices were created. Table 7 presents the matrix highlighting supportive values, using 50% as threshold.

Inspection of this matrix suggests that B_3 is largely supportive of all pillars.

	B1	B2	B3	B4	B5	B6	B7	B8
A1	50%	10%	70%	70%	60%	10%	50%	60%
A2	60%	50%	60%	20%	90%	20%	40%	50%
A3	90%	70%	80%	10%	89%	40%	70%	0%
A4	10%	0%	50%	10%	20%	0%	10%	30%
A5	40%	20%	60%	50%	50%	20%	30%	40%

Table 7: Matrix showing supportive values

The presence of these supportive values is a good sign of the strength of the supply chain strategy; providing support is its lifeblood, its main purpose. It is also interesting to notice the *absence* of supportive values. For example, notice in Table 7 that B_6 (a principle stated as "Operate with the lowest working capital") is not providing support above the 50% threshold to any of the pillars. Admittedly, the 50% threshold was an arbitrarily selected value, but as a tool for comparing the relative strengths of the different principles, it shows that of all the principles from B_1 through B_8, the B_6 principle is the one that provides the least support to the pillars of the business strategy, based on the assessment of the experts.

A concept can provide support to others above it. But it can also provide no support, or even be detrimental to other concepts above it. Table 8 presents the matrix highlighting detrimental values, using 50% as threshold.

	B1	B2	B3	B4	B5	B6	B7	B8
A1	50%	60%	20%	30%	40%	80%	50%	40%
A2	40%	40%	30%	70%	10%	70%	60%	50%
A3	10%	10%	20%	30%	0%	60%	30%	70%
A4	70%	60%	50%	80%	60%	80%	90%	70%
A5	60%	50%	30%	50%	40%	50%	60%	50%

Table 8: Matrix showing detrimental values

Inspection of this matrix suggests that principle B_6 is largely detrimental to all the strategy pillars. This begs the question of whether B_6 is a sound principle to be at the core of the supply chain strategy. If you recall from the coherence evaluation above, B_6 was also at the center of a key conflict between competing objectives in the supply chain strategy.

Another insight that can be glimpsed from the Table 8 matrix is that all principles of the supply chain strategy seem to be detrimental to A_4, one of the pillars of Unit-X's business strategy, which reads "Pursue innovation on high margin niches". You may remember from our coverage evaluation above that one of the blind spots in Unit-X's supply chain strategy was innovation. This makes us wonder: if the principles of the supply chain strategy are not supporting the innovation pillar, and innovation seems to be a blind spot in the supply chain strategy, Unit-X's supply chain strategy is falling short in terms of innovation. This should be cause for concern.

Sufficiency

Sufficiency is evaluated by asking the individuals what objectives (e.g. concepts from higher levels) are not currently being sufficiently satisfied by the supply chain strategy. Are the strategy pillars being satisfied by the cumulative support they receive from the supply chain strategy principles? Are the supply chain strategy principles being satisfied by the cumulative support they receive from the supply chain strategy imperatives?

In the past we have used two different approaches to assess sufficiency. The first is very simple: during the interviews of the capture process, and during the evaluation process for other criteria, we listen for comments - grievances would be a better word - the experts may have regarding shortcomings of the supply chain, ways in which the supply chain is falling short of expectations. This has worked for evaluating the sufficiency of current supply chain strategies.

Example

An example of a sufficiency shortcoming comes from our Libica project. Libica's core strategy, as seen in the left-most concept of Figure 17, is to "Make our customer's business less complex and more cost effective." After considering the question, the team of experts agreed that this goal was not being fully satisfied by the cumulative support it receives from all the concepts under it: pillars, principles, imperatives, policies and choices.

&

Another approach to assessing sufficiency, which we have not tried yet in one of our projects but seems promising, is by means of questions, as we have used for other criteria above. For each concept X in a high-level, we would ask the question "To what extent is X being satisfied as an objective?" The answer choices could be as follows:

1. Yes! It is fully satisfied
2. Yes. It is mostly satisfied
3. It is partly satisfied
4. No. it is mostly unsatisfied
5. No! It is fully unsatisfied
6. I am not sure

The individual answers from the experts are aggregated and presented to the group for validation and discussion. This approach was used by two of our students in a master's thesis we advised. We intend to apply it in the next supply chain evaluation project we may conduct.

About the remaining criteria

The evaluation criteria that we have discussed above with detailed examples are the ones that were developed as part of the SC2020 Project. We have more experience using them for evaluation. The remaining criteria, namely external consistency, parsimony, riskiness, advantageousness and actionability, were proposed after those projects were completed.

It is possible, retroactively, to identify examples for these newer criteria based on the data from our past projects. For instance, to illustrate the criterion of **external consistency**, we could mention that in our project with Unit-X we found an external inconsistency between the firm's intention of retaining their market share in premium products mostly through high product quality (e.g. without heavy investment in product innovation), and the fact that the new premium products in their industry were all the result of innovation.

However, better examples can be obtained by applying the criteria explicitly and directly in the evaluation of a supply chain strategy in a project. Once new projects are conducted, the newer criteria will be applied and richer examples will be collected, which will be included in future editions of this text.

CHAPTER 8

reformulating your SCS

On page 10, we outlined the three basic challenges involved with rethinking your supply chain strategy (Figure 29). We mentioned that the *first challenge* was how to *assess* your current supply chain strategy. By this we meant both knowing what supply chain strategy you have in place and recognizing its strengths and weaknesses.

```
┌─────────────────────────┐     ┌─────────────────────────┐
│      Challenge 1        │     │      Challenge 2        │
│  Assess your current    │     │   Anticipate future     │
│  supply chain strategy  │     │  supply chain needs     │
└─────────────────────────┘     └─────────────────────────┘
              ⬇                              ⬇
              ┌─────────────────────────┐
              │      Challenge 3        │
              │   Craft an improved     │
              │  supply chain strategy  │
              └─────────────────────────┘
```

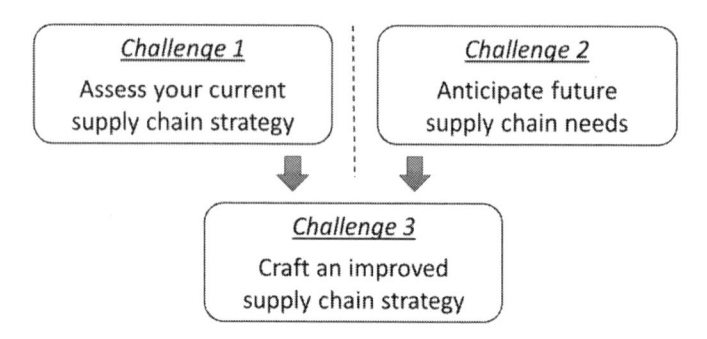

Figure 29. The basic challenges of rethinking a supply chain strategy

By now it should be clear that overcoming this first challenge is the goal behind the techniques presented in the previous chapters. Our method to capture the current supply chain strategy of an organization and to evaluate its strengths and weaknesses have proven useful aids to assessing existing supply chain strategies. This takes care of Challenge 1. The *second challenge* we discussed was how to anticipate the future supply chain needs that the organization may encounter. We mentioned that these future needs will depend, in part, on factors beyond the organization's control, such as the market and the industry in which the company will compete, or – in the case of not-for-profit organizations – the environment in which they will operate. We called these *external elements* (page 30) and mentioned they include *guidelines from the parent organization*, as well as *local factors*, i.e. variables that are beyond the control, but not beyond the influence, of the organization, and *driving forces*, i.e. variables that are beyond both the control and influence of the organization.

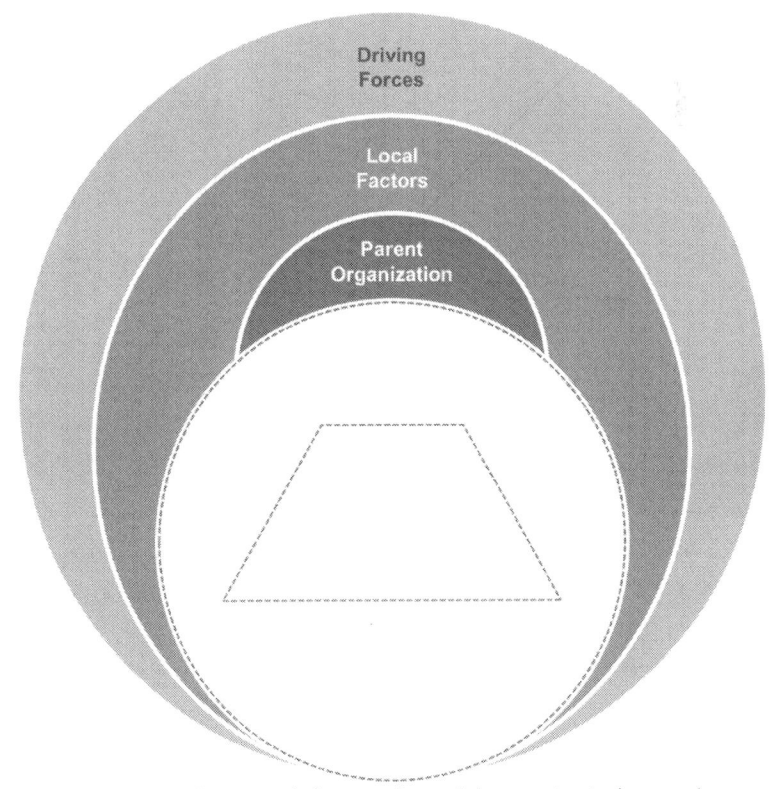

Figure 30: The external elements: beyond the organization's control

Local factors and driving forces have a significant effect on the future needs of the organization and the supply chain. Our colleague Dr. Shardul

Phadnis has written at length about how a technique known as *scenario planning* can be used to anticipate the future effects of driving forces (DF) and local factors (LF) on a supply chain strategy. In a scenario planning exercise for a business unit, for example, the industry and larger business environment is explored to identify major driving forces that are changing, while the market is scanned to identify local factors that may be either changing on their own or may be impacted by the driving forces.

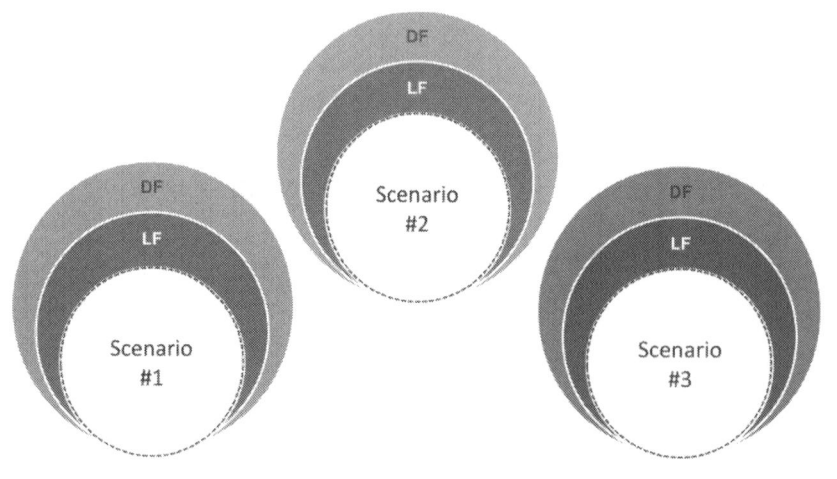

Figure 31: Scenario planning explores possibilities of DFs and LFs

By considering multiple plausible yet challenging combinations of the variations in driving forces and local factors, a set of scenarios can be concocted (Figure 31), each one pulling the mind of the manager in a particular direction. The implications of each scenario on the business can be considered, and robust implications can be identified. A subset composed of the robust driving forces and local factors can also be extracted. For more details on using scenario planning for supply chain strategizing, the reader is referred to the doctoral dissertation of Dr. Shardul Phadnis, *"Influencing managerial cognition and decisions using scenarios for long-range planning"* (MIT, 2012).

When we are rethinking a supply chain strategy for a time horizon that extends far into the future, a conscientious use of scenario planning can help an organization overcome Challenge 2. But it is not always necessary: for example, when we are rethinking a supply chain strategy to fix more immediate problems, with a mid-term horizon in mind, conducting a formal scenario planning exercise may not be necessary. In those cases, a sound, agreed-upon overall strategy, along with a clear understanding of the present environment of the organization, should suffice.

Finally, as we mentioned before, the **third challenge** is to craft an improved supply chain strategy for the present and the future. This new supply chain strategy, we argued, must support the expected future strategy of the organization, and be able to function in the future environment of the organization as envisioned in the scenario planning exercise. At the same time, this new supply chain strategy should retain or improve all the good features of the current supply chain strategy as identified in the evaluation, while fixing as many of its weaknesses as possible. We argued that this triple goal of fully supporting a new set of objectives while at the same time alleviating – or eliminating – the current shortcomings of the supply chain strategy and avoiding unnecessary changes to the current state, is not an easy one.

Progressive Formulation

Below we present our approach to reformulating the supply chain strategy of an organization. We call this approach *Progressive Formulation*.

Who is involved

To conduct a Progressive Formulation exercise, we will need a team of experts, a senior leader to serve as sponsor, and a neutral facilitator.

The team. Progressive Formulation is conducted by a team of experts, with the help of a neutral facilitator. The team of experts should be familiar with the outcomes of the capture and evaluation exercises. If a scenario planning exercise was conducted, they should be familiar with it as well. They should have a working knowledge of the business, market and industry, and should be willing to engage in the formulation exercise with an open mind and a positive, constructive attitude.

The sponsor. Progressive Formulation may be taxing, and it has a warm-up period before things click into place. To keep the team of experts engaged until the purpose of the exercise becomes clear, it helps to count with the leadership of a senior person that can serve as sponsor of the project, and who can champion it to keep the team engaged.

The facilitator. As before, an external and neutral facilitator with no skin in the game will be in charge of running the exercise. It is important that this facilitator does not answer or report to – formally – to the sponsor, and is seen as an independent party, an honest broker to help the team navigate the complex task of reformulating their supply chain strategy.

Figure 32: Team of experts doing Progressive Formulation

Required Inputs

The starting point for the reformulation is the current supply chain strategy of the organization. Therefore, one of the required inputs for the exercise is the output from the capture exercise, the FSM, which characterizes – in an activity-based manner – the current state of affairs. Another input is the result of the evaluation exercise. Knowing what is right and what is wrong with the current supply chain strategy will make it easier for the team to retain as many of the strong points of the current supply chain strategy as possible, while allowing them to modify the weaker ones. The extent to which the current state is retained will depend on how drastic are the changes needed for the new supply chain strategy.

A third input that should be provided to the team is a clear statement of the overall strategy of the organization, composed at a minimum of a core strategy statement and a set of strategy pillars that elaborate on it. Finally, if the reformulation is done for a long time horizon and a scenario planning exercise was conducted, the insights derived from it should also be provided to the team, in order to be considered during the reformulation of the new supply chain strategy. These last two inputs (external factors and overall strategy) are shown in terms of our model in Figure 33.

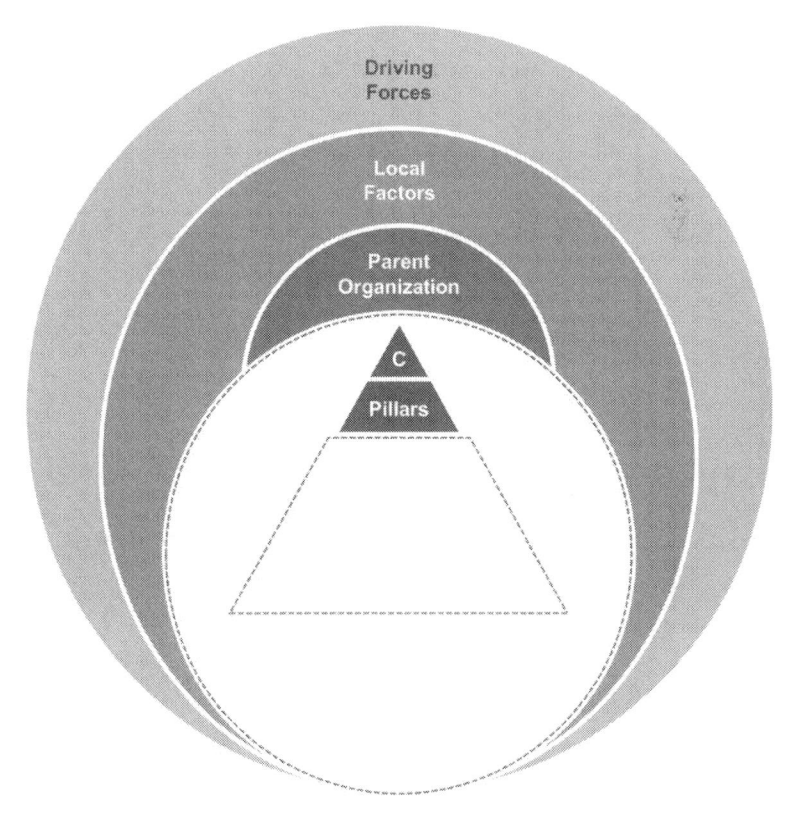

Figure 33: Starting point for Progressive Formulation

Steps

Progressive Formulation starts at the highest level of abstraction that will be reformulated. The team of experts is gathered in a well-lit room, with the sponsor and facilitator. The room's walls are wide, accessible and clear of obstacles, so that people can either post their ideas in pieces of paper or (if walls are whiteboard) write them down directly on the wall.

Guided by the facilitator, the team will do the following tasks.

> ***For each level***, *do Steps 1 through 6:*
>
> ***Step 1: Identify relevant areas of decision***
> Using the prerequisites as input, the team identifies the areas of decision that matter at this level of abstraction. Identifying all the relevant areas of decision is a first step towards satisfying the coverage criterion.

From the perspective of the working model, the objective of the Progressive Formulation exercise is to populate the supply chain strategy (e.g. the space within the dotted line polygon of Figure 33). Towards this goal, a useful first step is to demarcate the *Thematic Range* of the discussion by identifying a list of areas that must be addressed by the new supply chain strategy. These thematic areas that must be addressed by the new supply chain strategy are what we call the **areas of decision**. Areas of decision are the answer to the question, "What should our supply chain strategy talk about?" A good area identifies a topic (e.g. "Inventory" is a good area), without necessarily pointing towards a preferred direction (e.g. "Lower Inventory Levels" is not a good area, since it points towards a preference.) Areas of decision are placeholders across the thematic range (Figure 34.)

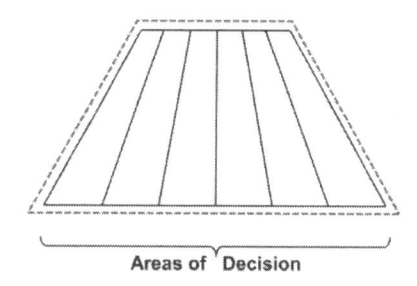

Figure 34: Areas of decision as placeholders across the thematic range

Areas of decision fall, in broad terms, under two categories:

- *Areas of interest* are the themes that interest us and in terms of which we define success, but that do not necessarily belong to anybody in particular, being more of a shared responsibility for the whole organization. Areas of Interest from projects past are: Cost, Quality, Service, Visibility, Flexibility, Traceability, Resilience, Efficiency, and Sustainability.
- *Areas of activity* are the themes that occupy us. They describe a type of activity for which someone is given responsibility. Areas of Activity from projects past are: Procurement, Manufacturing, Sales, Transportation, Warehousing, Marketing, Customer Service, Inventory Management, and Information Management.

In some cases, the distinction between an area of interest and an area of activity is somewhat arbitrary: for example, Quality is an area of interest, but quality control is an area of activity. These cases occur when the organization has already assigned responsibility for that area of interest to a particular party or group within the organization.

Some of the areas of decision may be grouped by theme into a hierarchy of super-areas, areas and sub-areas. For example, under the area "Costs", the team could place sub-areas like "Transportation Costs", "Procurement Costs", "Manufacturing Costs", "Warehousing Costs" etc. As a rule of thumb, based on previous projects, the team should strive to identify between three and five areas of decision for each Pillar. So, for a business strategy with four Pillars, the team should identify between 12 and 20 Areas of Decision (including areas and sub-areas).

Step 2: Sequence the areas of decision

The team decides how to sequence these areas for decision-making. This is done based on the relationships of precedence and dependency that may exist among them, and their relevance for achieving the overall strategy.

Once the areas of decision have been identified and listed, the team is asked to determine the sequence in which these areas will be considered.

The sequence is determined on the basis of both precedence and relevance. *Precedence* refers to the relationships of dependency that may exist between decisions made within given areas. For example, it makes little sense to make a decision in the area of Information Management until we have decided what we want to do in other areas, like Inventory or Customer Service. In general, *areas of interest* are given precedence over *areas of activity*. *Relevance* refers to the relative importance that attention to an area has for satisfying the overall strategy. For example, for a given business strategy, Quality may be more relevant than Cost.

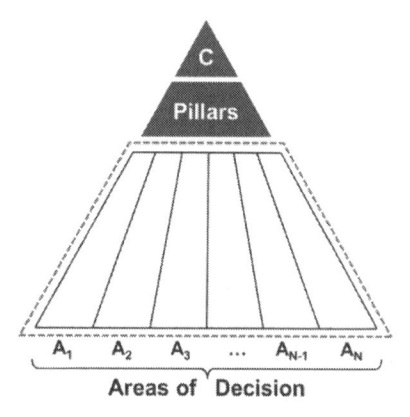

Figure 35: Sequenced areas of decision

Sequencing the areas for decision making is not the same as determining how valuable an area is to an organization or its public image. Teams often struggle to determine a sequence for making decisions along the areas, because they mistake this *sequencing* with a *ranking* of the areas based on their importance. There is a tendency, for example, to push areas like "Environmental Impact" or "Workplace Safety" to the front of the line, simply because leaving them for the end of the list makes them look like an afterthought, as if they mattered less than other areas.

However, *sequencing* and *ranking* are different tasks. A useful analogy to understand this difference is to compare the sequencing of the areas of decision with the "right of way" of cars in an all-way stop. Since all the areas of decision will have a chance to "move forward", the sequencing is not about eliminating some areas in favor of others. Instead, it is about establishing an order in which we want to *make decisions* regarding these areas. Because of the layer-by-layer approach of progressive formulation, it is possible to ensure that every area – even the last one in the sequence – gets its say in the new strategy. Ensuring a minimal environmental impact and maintaining high levels of workplace safety can be achieved even if these were the two last areas in the decision-making sequence above.

Then, for each area:
Once the areas have been identified and sequenced, the team will do Steps 3 through 5 for each area, working one area at a time, and starting with the first area in the sequence at the current level.

Step 3: Assess the current concept
If the current SCS has a concept for this area and level, the team evaluates it in terms of the evaluation criteria. If the team is satisfied with the current concept, they can skip Steps 4 and 5, and go to the next area.

Step 4: Generate several new concepts
Generation is about bringing innovative and creative thinking into the strategizing process. The team is asked to generate new concepts, as alternatives to the current concept in this area and level.

Step 5: Select the best concept
Selection is about bringing rigorous and selective thinking into the process. The team selects the best concept for this area and level - in terms of the evaluation criteria - from among those available.

Go to next area
Once a concept has been agreed upon for this area, we move to the next area in the sequence, and repeat steps 3, 4 and 5 for that area. This process is repeated until all the areas in this level have been addressed.

The purpose of Step 3 is to avoid unnecessary changes. For each area of decision and level of abstraction, the team discusses whether the current concept satisfies the evaluation criteria presented in Chapter 6. This is akin to asking: "Is the current concept good enough, or should we try to do better?" If the criteria are satisfied, the concept can be kept, and Steps 4 and 5 can be skipped.

The purpose of Step 4 is to innovate: since it has been determined by the team that they could do better, a concept needs to be to found. Step 4 is about proposing as many new good ideas as possible regarding how to improve this part of the supply chain strategy. The facilitator should foster innovative, and creative thinking when facilitating this step.

The purpose of Step 5 is selection: the goal is to select the best concept among the alternatives to replace the weak or blind spots of the current supply chain strategy, in a manner that is internally consistent and strategically aligned with the business strategy.

In order to be selected, a concept should be (a) *clear*, (b) *feasible* in the given context and environment, (g) more *supportive* of the concepts above it and of the overall strategy than the alternatives, and (c) more *parsimonious* in providing that level of support than the alternatives. It should also be not only (d) *compatible* with every other concept that has already been selected or retained, but also (e) more *coherent* (e.g. less detrimental to) and if possible, (f) more *synergistic* with all other concepts already selected or retained than the alternatives.

Step 6: Verify level-wide sufficiency

When Steps 1 through 5 have been done for all areas in the current level, we examine whether the concepts at that level are sufficient to satisfy the ones in the level above. If they are not, revisit Steps 1 through 5 as needed. It is possible to modify the existing concepts and/or to add new concepts in the areas, in a second pass, until sufficiency is achieved at this level.

Steps 1 – 5 are first applied at the level of Principles (Figure 36). Step 6 checks that, taken together, the Principles sufficiently satisfy the Pillars.

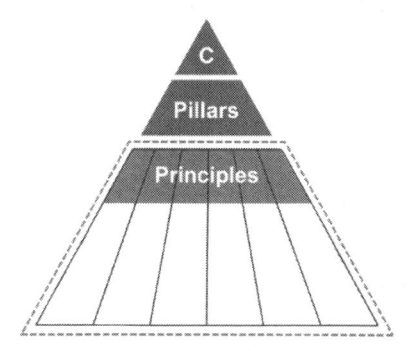

Figure 36: First, steps 1 through 6 are applied at the level of Principles

> **Go to next level**
> When we are done with that level, we move to the level below it. The same sequence of Steps 1 through 6 is repeated for that level.

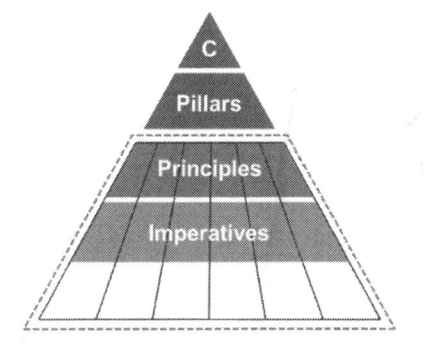

Figure 37: Then, steps 1 – 6 are applied to the level of Imperatives

Once we are done with the level of Principles, we move to the next level: steps 1 – 5 are repeated for the level of Imperatives (Figure 37). Step 6 checks that, taken together, the Imperatives sufficiently satisfy the Principles. Likewise, once we are done with the level of Imperatives, the same process is repeated for the level of Policies and Choices (Figure 38).

> When Steps 1 through 6 have been completed for all the relevant levels of abstraction, the Progressive Formulation exercise is *complete*.

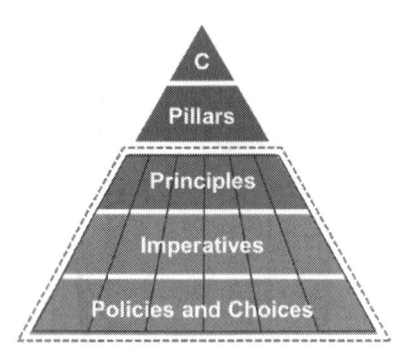

Figure 38: Finally, steps 1 – 6 are applied to the level of Policies and Choices

The resulting set of Principles, Imperatives, Policies and Choices constitutes our new supply chain strategy. What remains to be done is to decide how to *implement* these Policies and Choices in the field, in the form of Operational Practices across the supply chain. If it is deemed necessary, it is possible to continue the process of Steps 1 through 6 unto the next level of abstraction, that of Operational Practices. Although we expect it should work out fine, however, we have never done that in practice.

From Specification to Elaboration

From our first-hand experience – first creating and then applying the Progressive Formulation method in several projects – we have learned that, even though the sequence of steps used in each level of abstraction is the same, the *way* the sequence is applied --- more specifically, the way the concepts are generated and selected --- at each level is *not* the same. The nature of the concepts changes as we move down the strategy-operations continuum, and as such, the process of rethinking these concepts *feels* different from level to level.

Since concepts in the higher levels of abstraction (such as Principles and Imperatives) are more about purpose, generating and selecting concepts at these higher levels is about clearly stating the objectives that the business unit expects its supply chain strategy will fulfill. Taken together, these objectives specify the desired outcome, and thus provide a definition of success for the supply chain strategy. We refer to this stage of the Progressive Formulation as **specification**. Experts with strategic vision should be involved in this stage of the process.

Likewise, since concepts in the lower levels of abstraction (such as Policies and Choices, and Operational Practices) are more about practice, generating and selecting concepts at these lower levels is about deciding the means through which the supply chain strategy will support the objectives in higher levels. We refer to this stage of the Progressive Formulation as *elaboration*. At this stage we decide on means for execution, and experts with knowledge about the supply chain operations should be included in this stage of the process.

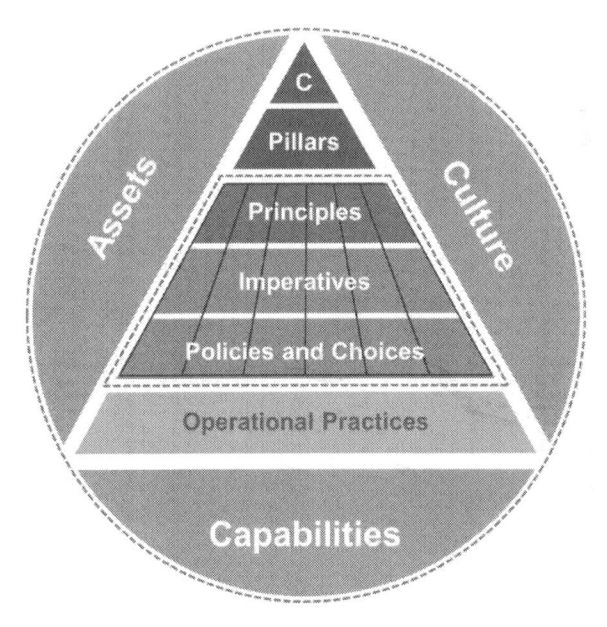

Figure 39: The enabling elements must support the new strategy

A word on implementation

To implement the new supply chain strategy, what remains is not only to determine how the Policies and Choices can be deployed as Operational Practices, but also how the existing Enabling Elements (e.g. Assets, Culture and Capabilities) must be changed to support the new supply chain strategy (Figure 39).

This may include developing new procedures, systems, roles within the organization, metrics, monitoring, etc. A roadmap for the changes is prepared. Implementation, however, is no longer a formulation problem, and thus lies beyond the scope of this method.

CHAPTER 9

reformulation examples

This chapter seeks to illustrate the Progressive Formulation method using examples from past projects. Before we do so, a brief *caveat* is in order. In the process of formalizing our methods in order to document them, they have been revised and refined. A full project to rethink the supply chain strategy of an organization is yet to be conducted after the latest version of the methods. Because of this, none of the projects completed to date can serve as a *canonical* example of Progressive Formulation, strictly following the steps as they were described in the previous chapter. Thus we will illustrate some aspects of Progressive Formulation using fragments from our project with Libica, and other aspects using fragments from a separate project. Both examples have been modified for confidentiality, and to better reflect the new method.

Example #1: Libica

In the project with Libica, after the capture and evaluation exercises were completed, we proceeded to conduct a reformulation exercise. Libica's Senior VP of Supply Chain served as sponsor and champion of the project, and one of the authors served as neutral facilitator. The same team of experts that participated in the capture and evaluation exercises (listed in Table 1) was also involved in the reformulation exercise. The team had at hand the outputs of the capture and reformulation. Since the supply chain strategy was being reformulated to address current issues, a visioning exercise was not conducted before the reformulation. Before the reformulation started, the Senior VP revised Libica's overall competitive strategy. The original Core and Pillars (shown before in Figure 20 in page 60) were revised to read as shown in Figure 40.

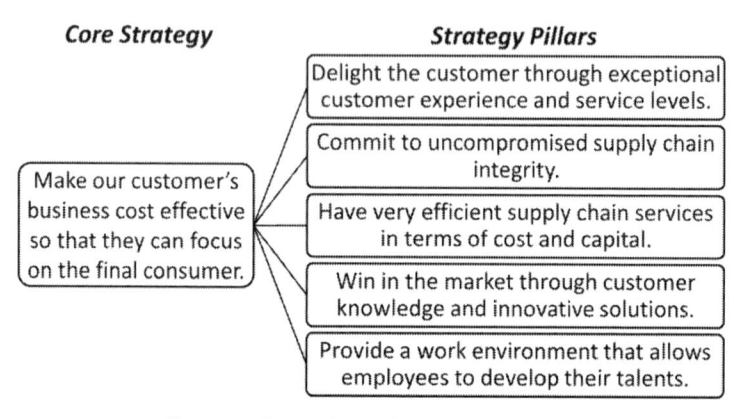

Core Strategy

Make our customer's business cost effective so that they can focus on the final consumer.

Strategy Pillars

Delight the customer through exceptional customer experience and service levels.

Commit to uncompromised supply chain integrity.

Have very efficient supply chain services in terms of cost and capital.

Win in the market through customer knowledge and innovative solutions.

Provide a work environment that allows employees to develop their talents.

Figure 40: Revised overall strategy for Libica

A word on levels of abstraction. As opposed to the canonical three levels (Principles, Imperatives, and Policies and Choices) shown in our model, the reformulation exercise with Libica was conducted using a simpler two-level model: *Objectives* and *Means*. **For the first level** of abstraction, that of *Objectives*, the team conducts Steps 1 through 6, as follows.

Step 1: Identify relevant areas of decision. The team identified the areas of decision that matter for their supply chain strategy at the level of objectives. As a starting point, they identified the areas of activity and interest addressed by the objectives in their current supply chain strategy, as described in the FSM shown in Figure 17 (page 42). These areas are:

- Outbound logistics: *How do we deliver?*
- Competency: *How do we compete? What is our focus?*
- Internal logistics: *How do we operate internally?*
- Profitability: *How do we make our profit?*
- National Accounts: *What do we do for national accounts?*

RETHINKING YOUR SUPPLY CHAIN STRATEGY | 109

- Specialty Accounts: *What do we do for specialty accounts?*
- Independents: *What do we do for independents?*
- Other customers: *What do we do for other customers?*
- Customer interaction: *How do we interact with the customer?*
- Collaboration with suppliers: *What kind, if any?*
- Management: *How do we manage our organization?*
- Workforce: *How do we interact with our workforce?*

The team added two areas that they considered were missing in their current supply chain strategy, so that they would be present in their new supply chain strategy (therefore improving two coverage shortcomings):

- Interaction with suppliers: *How do we interact with suppliers?*
- Collaboration with customers: *What kind, if any?*

Step 2: Sequence the areas of decision. Given the large number of areas, the team decided to identify common themes and group the areas into a hierarchy. They identified five common themes in the fifteen areas listed in Step 1. These five common themes are: (i) competition and profitability, (ii) serving the customers, (iii) managing the organization, (iv) interaction and collaboration, and (v) logistics.

I - Competition & profitability	1.	Profitability
	2.	Competency
II - Serving the customers	3.	National Accounts
	4.	Independents
	5.	Specialty
	6.	Other customers
III - Managing the organization	7.	Management
	8.	Workforce
IV - Interaction & collaboration	9.	Collaboration with customers
	10.	Collaboration with suppliers
	11.	Interaction with customers
	12.	Interaction with suppliers
V - Logistics	13.	Outbound logistics
	14.	Inbound logistics
	15.	Internal logistics

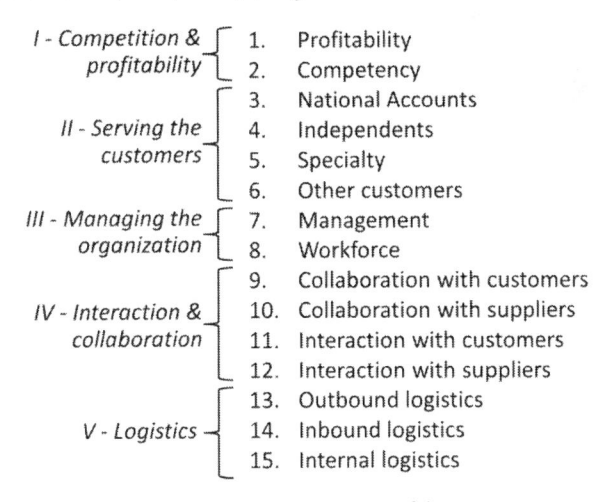

Table 9: Sequencing the areas of decision

The team then decided on a sequence of these five themes for making decisions, and after that, they sequenced the areas within each theme, as shown in Table 9. The team found these five themes to be more useful than the fifteen detailed areas. So the decision was made to use these five themes as the *new* areas of decision for the rest of the exercise.

The team now proceeds to do Steps 3 through 5 ***for each area***, working one area at a time, starting with Area I: "Competition and Profitability".

Step 3: Assess the current concept

Based on the FSM from the capture exercise, the facilitator prepared a summary of what the current SCS has in place for this area at the level of objectives. This summary was provided to the team, and read as follows:

> "Today Libica makes its profit through distribution. As part of its focus on efficiency, Libica tries to eliminate or reduce waste in distribution. Libica tries to improve profitability through better customer and product mix: adding profitable customers and increasing profitable sales through existing customers. Libica wants to find ways to make added-value services one of its core competencies and a source of profit."

The team was asked to consider whether they were satisfied with what Libica had in place. They felt they could do better, so steps 4 and 5 were conducted next.

Step 4: Generate several new concepts

The experts were asked, individually at first, to propose new ideas of objectives that Libica can pursue in this area. Eighteen different ideas were gathered from different experts. A summary was prepared and shared – without attribution – with the whole team for consideration.

Step 5: Select the best concept

The team selects the best concept for this area and level – in terms of the evaluation criteria – from among those available. It was the following:

> *Compete by being a supply chain solutions provider. Change the game: move away from price, and into value and solutions.*

Once a concept (only one!) has been agreed upon for this area, we move to the next area in the sequence, Area II: "Serving the customers," and repeat steps 3, 4 and 5 for that area. The team assessed the current concept for Area II (*Step 3*) and thought they could do better. They proposed fifteen new ideas (*Step 4*). From these, they selected the concept (*Step 5*) they considered was the best in terms of the evaluation criteria:

> *Offer several service-level categories, with different service options attached to cost. Allow customers to choose the category/options they want, and suggest to them what category we think would better serve them.*

After this concept has been agreed upon for this area, we move to the next area in the sequence and repeat Steps 3 through 5. For Area III: "Managing the organization," the summary of the status quo read thus:

> *"Today in Libica management is done through clear and well communicated objectives. A high-level road map is developed and followed. Those in a leadership position are taught to be metric-driven and open to communication and change. Managers are encouraged to work cross-functionally to satisfy the customer's needs. Today Libica seeks to educate and empower its workforce, and to develop its capabilities."*

The team assessed the current concept for Area III (*Step 3*) and decided to retain this *status quo*, but to do more in addition to it. So they proposed fourteen new ideas (*Step 4*) to be done in addition to what they do now. Among these, they selected the best concept (*Step 5*) in terms of the evaluation criteria, to be done "*in addition to the goals being pursued today*":

> *Learn how to use metrics wisely.*

This process is repeated for Areas IV and V.

Step 6: Verify level-wide sufficiency

Now that Steps 1 through 5 have been done for all five areas at the level of objectives, the team examined whether the objectives selected so far are sufficient to satisfy the five pillars stated in Figure 40. The team deemed the pillars were not yet satisfied.

A second pass of concept assessment (*Step 3*), concept generation (*Step 4*) and concept selection (*Step 5*) was conducted at this level. In this second pass, new concepts were added in each one of the five areas of decision. After this second pass was done, another check for level-wide sufficiency was carried out (*Step 6*). The team found the pillars were still not satisfied. So, a third pass of *Steps 3* through *5* was conducted at this level, in which concepts were added to areas I, II and IV. After this third pass was completed, another check for level-wide sufficiency was done (*Step 6*). At this point, the team assess that the five pillars were satisfied. Table 10 shows the objectives that the team selected for all areas except Area IV. Having achieved sufficiency at the level of objectives, the team moved to the next level: the means to support these objectives.

For the second level of abstraction, that of *Means*, the team conducts again Steps 1 through 6. When the team of experts deems that level-wide sufficiency has been achieved (i.e. when the experts think that the support provided by all the selected means sufficiently satisfies the objectives in the level above them) the Progressive Formulation is complete.

Example #2: Convenience Stop

The Libica example illustrated the mechanics of Progressive Formulation within a level. However, we would like to finish this chapter with a second example, the output from another project done with a convenience store franchise that we will call *Convenience Stop*. Their Progressive Formulation was conducted at two levels: *Objectives* and *Decisions*. The output for this project is rich in detail for both levels, and a better example of what the output of Progressive Formulation looks like today.

Area of Decision I: ***Competition and profitability***
- Objective: *Compete by being a supply chain solutions provider. Change the game: move away from price, and into value and solutions.*
- Objective: *Make our profit by helping our customers to become profitable, and then sharing this profit that we have created for them.*
- Objective: *Explore new markets in areas that look promising for development.*

Area of Decision II: **Serving the customers**
- Objective: *Offer several service-level categories, with different service options attached to cost. Allow customers to choose the [one] they want, and suggest to them what category we think would better serve them.*
- Objective: *For value-oriented customers, work to better understand what the customer wants, what they value, what they're struggling with, what's going to help them. Develop the capability of looking at the customer and helping them run their business better.*
- Objective: *For large customers, offer tailored supply chain solutions, and charge accordingly. Distinguish our pricing and costing models, so that we can have greater flexibility in our offerings. This requires an informed way to cost out our services, based upon activity.*

Area of Decision III: **Managing the organization**

In addition to the goals being pursued today, do the following:
- Objective: *Learn how to use metrics wisely.*
- Objective: *Align the compensation of personnel whose decisions and actions impact the SC, at least in part, with the overall profitability.*

...

Area of Decision V: **Logistics**

In addition to what we do today, do the following:
- Objective: *Invest in capabilities to deliver.*
- Objective: *Find a way to deliver multiple service levels out of the same logistics facilities.*

Table 10: Areas and objectives from Libica's reformulation (Area IV not shown)

What follows are the areas, objectives and decisions that were selected for thirteen out of twenty-two areas of decision during Convenience Stop's Progressive Formulation exercise.

Area of Decision 01: **Supply Chain Quality**
- *Objective: Continually improve our rate of perfect delivery*
  - *Decision: Continually improve fill rate to stores*
  - *Decision: Ensure the product arrives in the highest quality conditions possible*
  - *Decision: Deliver to stores within the promised window*
- *Objective: Protect the quality of product through the SC*
  - *Decision: Use appropriate equipment to handle products (especially frozen food and fragile items)*
  - *Decision: Ensure people handle the product appropriately*
- *Objective: Be invisible to the guest*
  - *Decision: Timing deliveries to non-peak hours*
  - *Decision: Ensure appropriate delivery behavior*

Area of Decision 03: **Supply Chain Efficiency**
- *Objective: Make better use of resources in our SC*
  - *Decision: Identify and reduce the waste in the supply chain*
- *Objective: Reduce the cost of delivery, subject to quality requirements*
  - *Decision: Find opportunities to improve transportation*
  - *Decision: Route outbound distribution more efficiently*
  - *Decision: Look for improvement opportunities in front-haul and backhaul in inbound transportation*
- *Objective: Maintain efficient movement of goods within the SC*
  - *Decision: Avoid 'dead items' in the supply chain*
  - *Decision: Increase the number of inventory turns*

Area of Decision 05: **Supply Chain Flexibility**
- *Objective: Adapt the supply chain to changing store and guest needs and expectations*
  - *Decision: Design the warehouses and transportation for adaptability*
  - *Decision: Develop the ability to recognize the new needs of the customers*
- *Objective: Be able to respond to emergency needs*

- o   Decision: Develop Business Continuity Plan
- Objective: Retain the ability to adapt the supply chain to changing regulatory requirements
    - o   Decision: Develop a Regulatory Compliance Role

Area of Decision 06: **Product Assortment**
- Objective: Make sure the supply chain is considered in product assortment decision
    - o   Decision: Grow awareness throughout the company of the impact of product assortment on the supply chain
    - o   Decision: Have a senior voice with veto power in product assortment decisions

Area of Decision 08: **Supply Chain Scalability**
- Objective: Retain the ability to ramp up the SC's capacity to support demand as needed
    - o   Decision: Obtain real estate or buildings with capability/space to expand when needed
    - o   Decision: Build in options for scalability in our SC systems, processes and infrastructure
- Objective: Make sure the supply chain is considered in all major decisions
    - o   Decision: Have a senior voice with veto power in all major decisions, including mergers and acquisitions (M&A)

Area of Decision 09: **Human Factor**
- Objective: Have a competent workforce
    - o   Decision: Hire high quality, capable people for all functions
    - o   Decision: Provide our employees with targeted, role-specific training
    - o   Decision: Provide constructive feedback to our employees
- Objective: Establish a common culture, based on sound leadership principles
    - o   Decision: Train and develop 'servant leadership' qualities in our personnel
- Objective: Have a diverse workforce
    - o   Decision: Institute hiring practices that lead to a diverse workforce
    - o   Decision: Promote diversity of thought in our organization

Area of Decision 10: **Safety and Security**
- *Objective: Provide a safe and secure working environment*
  - *Decision: Enforce rules and regulations for safety and security, with incentives*
  - *Decision: Develop internal policies and identify relevant safety regulations*
- *Objective: Provide, to the extent possible, a tamper-proof environment for our supply chain*
  - *Decision: Continuously monitor (as in 'surveillance') our supply chain*
  - *Decision: If a product is compromised, prevent further movement towards guests*
- *Objective: Provide, to the extent possible, a theft-proof environment*
  - *Decision: Continuously monitor (as in 'surveillance') our supply chain (same as above: this serves two objectives)*

Area of Decision 14: **Inventory Management**
- *Objective: Balance the cost of warehouse with the cost of potential outages*
  - *Decision: Be able to estimate the opportunity cost of lost sales*
  - *Decision: Develop the ability to analyze and control the relative costs of warehousing and lost sales*
- *Objective: Achieve timely visibility of inventory in our supply chain*
  - *Decision: Track inventory at key points of the supply chain, with timely updates*

Area of Decision 18: **Sourcing and Procurement**
- *Objective: Procure the best value goods and services in a timely manner*
  - *Decision: Leverage the scale of the business to maximize the profit of a purchase*
  - *Decision: Employ strategic sourcing techniques: deal buys, forward buys, diverting, etc.*
  - *Decision: Have the right team in sourcing, made up of knowledgeable, strategically-minded people*

Area of Decision 19: **Warehousing**
- *Objective: Maintain and continually improve warehouse operations*

- Decision: Understand how warehouse operations are done today.
- Decision: Identify opportunities for improvement in warehouse operations.
- Decision: Implement these improvements in the operations of the warehouses.

Area of Decision 20: **Inbound Transportation**
- Objective: Ensure the most efficient inbound transportation solution that meets our quality requirements
    - Decision: Encourage the use of full truck transportation whenever possible.
    - Decision: Schedule inbound deliveries and coordinate with supplier and warehouse.
    - Decision: Employ the purchase order as a communication piece: allow the buyer to include comments. Include delivery conditions and considerations in it (due dates, etc.)

Area of Decision 21: **Risk Management**
- Objective: Anticipate, and prepare for, disruptions to the supply chain
    - Decision: Identify the risks that could affect the supply chain, and estimate their probability
    - Decision: Develop and test mitigating responses to the risks that have been identified.
    - Decision: Do the things stated above on an ongoing basis.

Area of Decision 22: **Customer Service**
- Objective: Resolve customer service problems in a timely manner
    - Decision: Create our own customer service organization, with a well-defined role within the supply chain
    - Decision: Build integration between the SC customer service center and other customer service centers

CHAPTER 10

connecting the dots

Let us circle back to the first issue we raised in this text: the complex nature of supply chain strategizing. In the first pages of Chapter 1 we argued that rethinking the supply chain strategy of an organization presents practitioners at least three distinct, but interrelated, challenges.

```
┌─────────────────────┐     ┌─────────────────────┐
│    Challenge 1      │     │    Challenge 2      │
│ Assess your current │     │  Anticipate future  │
│ supply chain strategy│    │ supply chain needs  │
└─────────────────────┘     └─────────────────────┘
             ↓                         ↓
            ┌─────────────────────┐
            │    Challenge 3      │
            │  Craft an improved  │
            │ supply chain strategy│
            └─────────────────────┘
```

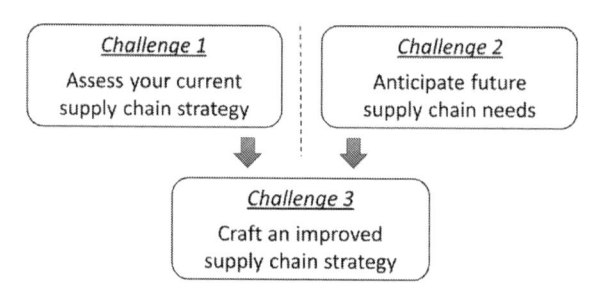

Figure 41: The basic challenges of rethinking a supply chain strategy

Let us explain now how our approach to supply chain strategizing – as described in Chapters 3 through 9 – addresses each one of the three basic challenges. (As we do so, we will refer in parenthesis to the seven *fundamental tasks* that – as mentioned in Chapter 2 – must take place in order to rethink the supply chain strategy of an organization.)

Challenge 1, as we mentioned, is to assess the current supply chain strategy. Our response to this challenge is twofold.

First, we conduct a *capture* exercise. We have developed an approach, that we call Functional Strategy Mapping (FSM) Method, to explicitly articulate the current supply chain strategy of a firm in the form of a conceptual map. This map is thoroughly grounded on factual activities, and shows the relationships of activities with their immediate goals, and of these with more abstract goals. This method is presented and illustrated in Chapters 4 and 5. (The capture exercise is a way to execute *fundamental task #4*.) A necessary step before the capture exercise can be conducted is to define a clear scope of what will be included in the supply chain strategy map. (This takes care of *fundamental task #1*.)

Second, we conduct an *evaluation* exercise. We have developed a set of evaluation criteria, which are applicable to the organization irrespective of its industry or field of concern. We have developed mechanisms to apply many of these evaluation criteria for the evaluation of the current supply chain strategy of the organization. The evaluation criteria and their use are discussed in Chapters 6 and 7. The result of the evaluation is a diagnostic of the strengths and weaknesses of the current supply chain strategy, and indicate what can be kept and what must change for the future. (The evaluation exercise is a way to execute *fundamental task #5*.)

The capture exercise provides a solid foundation for the subsequent evaluation of the current supply chain strategy. Both serve then as a starting point for the elaboration of a new and improved supply chain strategy that better serves the future needs of the organization. We have argued that developing a factual understanding of what your supply chain strategy is today takes time and effort, but it is the best way to ground the subsequent strategy reformulation in the reality of the organization.

Challenge 2 – relevant mostly when considering *medium-* and *long-term* horizons, but not so much for the short-term – is knowing what new future expectations we want to set for the supply chain strategy. Our response to this challenge is to conduct a visioning exercise. Our tool of choice for visioning is a method for scenario planning that was tailored to supply chain strategizing, as presented in Phadnis (2012). The philosophy behind using a scenario planning approach has at its core the premise that it is possible to prepare for the effects of unpredictable future events. This method calls for generating a set of complementary and individually challenging, plausible and relevant scenarios, and then for the distillation of insights regarding the implications that different futures may have for the supply chain. These implications – some robust, others contingent on future developments – will be priceless in informing the supply chain strategy formulation later on. (This visioning exercise takes care of *fundamental task #5*.)

Challenge 3 is to know what our supply chain strategy should look like, given our future expectations. Our response to this challenge is to conduct a strategy reformulation exercise using a method we call Progressive Formulation, as discussed in Chapter 8. The starting point for this reformulation is the assessment of the current state, an understanding of the future needs (from the visioning exercise), and an agreed-upon overall strategy for the organization.

Progressive Formulation starts by defining the areas of decision that will be included in the reformulation process. (This, again, addresses *fundamental task #1*.)

The early stages of the reformulation consist of stating a set of strategic objectives for the supply chain (Principles and Imperatives). These objectives are the answer to the question: what do we expect our supply chain to be able to do moving forward? The process of defining these objectives is what we call *specification*. Its importance lies in the fact that - taken together - these strategic objectives for the supply chain represent the *definition of success* for a supply chain strategy. (Specification takes care of *fundamental task #3*.)

The way we reformulate our supply chain strategy alternates between generating new ideas (which takes care of *fundamental task #6*) and selecting the best among them (which takes care of *fundamental task #7*).

Even though implementation is beyond the scope of the strategy formulation process, implementing a new supply chain strategy generated through our approach is relatively straightforward: since both the current and the new supply chain strategies are articulated in a similar manner, it is easy to identify areas that require change. Sequencing those changes in a logical manner allows the organization to develop a roadmap for the implementation of the new supply chain strategy. Some ideas on implementation were presented at the end of Chapter 8.

Finally, in the last few pages of Chapter 1 we presented a list of seven prescriptions to help you reduce the complexity of rethinking your supply chain strategy. We promised that, by the time you were done reading this text, you would have received guidance regarding how to apply each one of these prescriptions. Table 11 summarizes how each one of the seven fundamental tasks outlined before are in line with the seven prescriptions to reduce complexity.

	Rx #1	Rx #2	Rx #3	Rx #4	Rx #5	Rx #6	Rx #7
Task #1	✓						
Task #2			✓			✓	✓
Task #3				✓			
Task #4		✓				✓	✓
Task #5					✓		✓
Task #6					✓		
Task #7					✓		

Table 11: Relationship between tasks and prescription

- By defining a reasonable scope (*Task #1*), the extent of the supply chain to be considered in the strategizing effort can be kept within manageable bounds, which reduces the objective complexity of the system (*Rx #1*).
- By clearly articulating the current supply chain strategy (Task #4), your ability to understand the system is increased (*Rx #2*).
- By anticipating the future needs of the supply chain through visioning (*Task #2*), you reduce the likelihood and impact of surprises, which tends to reduce the time pressure in decision making (*Rx #3*).
- By stating the objectives that the supply chain strategy is expected to

support (*Task #3*), you clearly specify the desired end state (*Rx #4*).
- By identifying conflicts through evaluation (*Task #5*) and reformulating the strategy to include only internally consistent concepts (*Tasks #6 and #7*), you address conflicts between partial goals (*Rx #5.*)
- By developing a better understanding of the current supply chain strategy (*Task #4*) and its flaws (*Task #5*), as well as of the driving forces and local factors that shape its environment (*Task #2*), we get more complete information about the system (*Rx #7*) and increase our knowledge about its structure (*Rx #6*).

∽

It has taken us a whole decade of collaborative research with organizations to *rethink* from scratch the way in which *we*, as academics, approach the problem of supply chain strategy and strategizing. No doubt, the list of questions we have identified so far is incomplete, and for sure the answers we have advanced for those questions are imperfect. But we are convinced that the new approach to supply chain strategizing that we propose in this text – flawed as it may be – represents a significant improvement over the currently predominant approach to the subject.

There is a long road ahead. In order to continue researching the subject of supply chain strategy, the twelve-year old Supply Chain 2020 Project at the Center for Transportation and Logistics has been transitioned into the newly created MIT Supply Chain Strategy Lab. With the help of partner companies and researchers, the SCS Lab will continue to explore key questions about supply chain strategy. If you are interested in finding out more about the MIT SCS Lab, or maybe even collaborating with us in a project, you can find our contact information in the copyright page.

In the meantime, it is our hope that this brief guide may prove useful as a starting point for practitioners looking to *rethink* the supply chain strategies of their organizations.

references

Andrews, K. R. (1991) "The concept of corporate strategy". In *Business Policy: Text and Cases*.

Dörner, Dietrich. (1983) "Heuristics and cognition in complex systems." In *Methods of Heuristics*.

Fine, Charles. (1998) *Clockspeed: Winning industry control in the age of temporary advantage*. Basic Books.

Fisher, Marshall. (1997) "What is the right supply chain for your product?" *Harvard Business Review* 75: 105-117.

Phadnis, Shardul. (2012) *Influencing managerial cognition and decisions using scenarios for long-range planning*. PhD Dissertation, MIT.

Porter, Michael. (1996) "What is strategy?" *Harvard Business Review*, 74(6), 61-78.

Roy, S. (2005) *World class supply chains in the computer industry*. Master Thesis, MIT.

Rumelt, Richard. (1979). "Evaluation of strategy: Theory and models." In *Strategic management: A new view of business policy and planning*.

Tilles, S. (1963). "How to Evaluate Corporate Strategy." *Harvard Business Review*, 41(4), 111-121.

index

actionability, 69
advantageousness, 69
areas of decision, 99
   areas of activity, 100
   areas of interest, 100
   sub-areas, 100
   super-areas, 100
articulation, 20, 33, 34, 41
   portrait analogy, 34
   vs categorization, 34
asking 'how?', 36
asking 'why?', 36, 44
assets, 28, 107
axes of complexity, 18
basic challenges, 9, 93
best practices, 16
   vs tailored practices, 16
bottom-up, 43, 44
capabilities, 28, 107
categorization, 33
clarity, 65, 74
   example, 74
clockspeed, 19
coherence, 66, 81
   example, 82
collective feedback
   on FSM, 62
compatibility, 66, 77
   example, 79
complex problem, 12
   features of, 11

   vs well-defined problem, 11
complexity, 7
   objective, 13
   subjective, 13
concept
   as building blocks, 35
   concept assessment, 102
   concept generation, 102
   concept selection, 102
conceptual elements, 27
conceptual map, 34, 36, 44
   how to read, 37
   levels in..., 36
   making a small..., 34
   meaning of lines, 36
   rotated, 44
   vertical axis, 38
conceptual system
   meaning, 34
consistency
   external, 67
   internal, 66
   levels of internal..., 66
core, 26, 43, 60
coverage, 40, 64, 71
   example, 72
culture, 28, 107
dimensions of strategizing, 23
driving forces, 31
elaboration, 106
enabling elements, 28, 107

evaluation, 21, 34, 63
  avoid early..., 41
evaluation criteria, 64
executed strategy, 43, 44
external consistency, 67
external elements, 29
external wisdom, 17
facilitator, 17, 97
feasibility, 65, 75
  example, 75
FSM Method, 46
Functional Strategy Map, 46
  as input to formulation, 97
  assembling, 61
  from Libica, 78
  from Unit-X, 73
  validating, 61
fundamental tasks, 18
generation, 21
hierarchical summary, 56
imperatives, 26
implementation, 22, 106
individual feedback
  on FSM, 61
inertial elements, 29
internal consistency, 65, 77
internal elements, 29
internal wisdom, 17
local factors, 31
nominal strategy, 43, 44, 60
operational practices, 26
parent organization, 30
parsimony, 68
partial maps
  building, 57
  combining, 59
  validation, 58
Phadnis, Shardul, 20, 31, 95
pillars, 26, 43, 60

policies and choices, 26, 56
precedence, 101
principles, 26
Progressive Formulation, 96
reformulation, 34
relevance, 101
riskiness, 69
Rumelt's Challenge, 63
scenarios, 20, 95
scoping, 18
selection, 21
sequencing, 100
  vs ranking, 101
specification, 20, 106
strategizing, 7
strategy-operations continuum, 24, 38
sufficiency, 68, 90
  example, 90
  level-wide, 103
supply chain strategy
  composition, 25
  definition, 23
supply-chain relevant, 24, 39
supply-demand dimension, 24
support, 68, 86
  example, 88
synergy, 67, 81
  example, 82
tailored practices, 16
taming complexity, 13
  prescriptions, 14
thematic range, 24, 28, 39, 40
top-down, 43
type-based vs specific, 15
types, 15, 33
validation
  of partial maps, 58
visioning, 19

Made in the USA
Middletown, DE
12 January 2018